THE PUBLIC SECTOR PIVOT

Eva —

Thanks so much for your support!

Kaitlyn Rentala

THE PUBLIC SECTOR PIVOT

HOW GEN Z WILL LEAD A RENAISSANCE OF PUBLIC SERVICE

KAITLYN RENTALA

NEW DEGREE PRESS

THE PUBLIC SECTOR PIVOT

How Gen Z Will Lead a Renaissance of Public Service

ISBN   978-1-63676-909-7   *Paperback*
            978-1-63676-973-8   *Kindle Ebook*
            978-1-63730-077-0   *Ebook*

"The time is always right to do what is right."

—MARTIN LUTHER KING JR.

CONTENTS

INTRODUCTION   **11**

PART 1.   **HOW DID WE GET HERE?**   **25**
CHAPTER 1.   BUSINESS INFLUENCE IN THE PUBLIC SECTOR   27
CHAPTER 2.   THE EFFICIENCY PERCEPTION:
MILLENNIALS VS. GEN Z   39

PART 2.   **WHAT ARE THE PROBLEMS WITH THE SYSTEM
NOW?**   **53**
CHAPTER 3.   ISSUES WITH THE PUBLIC SECTOR TALENT
PIPELINE   55
CHAPTER 4.   ISSUES WITH THE FEDERAL HIRING PROCESS   69
CHAPTER 5.   GOVERNMENT PAY   81

PART 3.   **WHERE DO WE GO FROM HERE?**   **99**
CHAPTER 6.   THE NEW PUBLIC SECTOR TALENT PIPELINE   101
CHAPTER 7.   THE CIVIC TECH MOVEMENT   115
CHAPTER 8.   HOW THE COVID-19 PANDEMIC WILL
CHANGE PUBLIC SERVICE   135

CONCLUSION   147
ACKNOWLEDGEMENTS   155
APPENDIX   159

To my parents: this book would not exist without you.

INTRODUCTION

———

Brandon Chin[1] is, by all accounts, the type of young talent government desperately tries to recruit.

The son of Chinese immigrants, Brandon grew up in Section 8 housing in Central New Jersey. Like many immigrant families, Brandon's parents highly prioritized education, and he thrived in school. He applied and was accepted into High Technology High School, a prestigious magnet school ranked the number one STEM school in the US by US News & World Report in 2020.[2] After graduating, Brandon went on to the Ivy League, attending the University of Pennsylvania.

While at Penn, Brandon further focused on science and technology, majoring in Mechanical Engineering and Applied Mechanics. He excelled in technical courses like Machine Learning and Python, won top awards in app-building competitions, and conducted research in a Nobel Physics Prize-winning lab.

———

1   Pseudonym at the request of interviewee.
2   "High Technology High School," *US News and World Report*, accessed September 04, 2020.

After graduating from Penn in 2017, Brandon—following the pathway typical of a talented college graduate—moved to New York City and took a job at a technology start-up called KeyMe as a data scientist. At this point in his life, Brandon's career path seemed set. He would do two years at KeyMe and then move to a larger technology company or possibly a hedge fund. Facebook and many hedge funds in New York had already come calling. It is, without a doubt, an American Dream story of success.

But that's not Brandon's story.

In 2019, after two years in the start-up world, Brandon wanted to make a change. He was restless and young, eager to pursue something larger than himself. So, he made a career move that seemed radical to his friends and family: entering politics.

The timing seemed right and consequential. "When Trump won in 2016, I felt like there was nothing I could do," Brandon remarked. "But I had been working for two years and I now had a very specific set of skills that were applicable. I had paid off all my student debt. I could afford to make the shift."

But ultimately, Brandon made the change out of a desire to do good; "I've always been pretty idealistic. *The West Wing* is one of my all-time favorite shows," he said with a laugh. "But really, I felt like I'd been fortunate in my own personal situation. I didn't come from much and I was now in a position to give back."

Going into politics was a function of passion and pure idealism.

Brandon's story is the story of Generation Z.

The story of Gen Z is one of passion. Idealism. Anger. Rage. Determination. Disdain of apathy. Although most Gen Zers can't even vote yet, they are revolutionizing civic engagement in the modern day. Members of Gen Z are those born after 1996, making it the first digital generation. Gen Zers have used their innate familiarity with social media to push for widespread societal change. For example, in the wake of the Parkland shooting that killed seventeen people, the students from Marjory Stoneman Douglas High School utilized Twitter, Instagram, and Snapchat to register hundreds of thousands of people to vote and organized the March for Our Lives movement to push for gun reform.[3] Thirteen-year-old Amariyanna Copeny, also known as "Little Miss Flint," uses Twitter to spread awareness about the water crisis in America and has supplied more than one million water bottles to Flint, Michigan in the wake of the Flint water crisis.[4] Seventeen-year-old Darnella Frazier recorded police officer Derek Chauvin murdering George Floyd and helped spark possibly the largest movement in United States history.[5]

From the March for Our Lives protests to climate change protests to the Black Lives Matter movement, young people

---

3 Li Cohen, "From TikTok to Black Lives Matter, how Gen Z is Revolutionizing Activism," *CBS News*, July 20,2020.

4 Ibid.

5 Larry Buchanan et al., "Black Lives Matter May Be the Largest Movement in US History," *New York Times*, July 3, 2020.

are beyond civically engaged; they're civically enraged. And they're ready to impact government for decades to come.

But not right now.

Currently, young people are severely underrepresented in public service. In the US, only 7 percent of federal government employees are under the age of thirty, compared to 23 percent in the private sector. The numbers are even worse in tech. Just 3 percent of the government's 84,097 tech specialists are under the age of thirty, while 14 percent of IT workers are over the age of sixty. In some agencies like the Department of Veteran Affairs, the number of tech specialists over sixty outnumber their under-thirty counterparts 19:1.[6]

These numbers alone are troubling, but combined with the fact that 25 percent of federal employees plan on retiring within the next five years, the lack of young people in government threatens the very health of the federal system.[7] Altogether, a staggering 150,000 federal employees are set to retire in the near future, leaving a gap of leadership and expertise in the federal government.[8]

The next decade will bring a slew of increasingly complex challenges: climate change, health care reform, and an

---

6   Jack Corrigan, "At One Civilian Agency, IT Pros Over 60 Years Old Outnumber Their Under 30 Year Colleagues 19 to One," *Nextgov*, October 1, 2018.

7   Mark Hensch, "A Quarter of Feds Plans on Retiring Within 25 Years," *Govloop*, October 30, 2018.

8   Ibid.

increasingly digitized world. To effectively tackle these pressing issues, we need the most effective government possible.

Public officials have started to take notice. When Barack Obama was running for president in 2008, he pledged to "make government cool again."[9] After the record youth voter turnout in the 2008 presidential election, President Obama sought to capitalize on youth momentum and recruit young people into public service.

The Obama Administration implemented several new measures to support national service, including creating over 4,500 new AmeriCorps opportunities, reforming the Peace Corps, and establishing the President's Task Force on Expanding National Service.

Furthermore, Obama brought Silicon Valley to Washington to attract young tech talent. During his tenure, Obama brought the digital revolution to the White House. He created the Office of the US Chief Technology Officer (CTO), appointing former Silicon Valley tech CEOs to the role. In 2012, the White House established the Presidential Innovation Fellows (PIF) program, which pairs tech entrepreneurs and innovators with federal government employees. Civic tech programs like the United States Digital Service, which serves as a tech start-up within the White House, and 18F, a digital service agency within the General Services Administration, quickly followed suit.

---

9   Ben Smith, "Obama Plans To 'Make Government Cool Again," *Politico*, September 11, 2008

Despite all of Obama's efforts, the number of individuals younger than thirty in the federal workforce actually fell during his tenure. According to the Office of Personnel Management (OPM), the percentage of new hires under thirty fell from 37 percent in 2011 to 35 percent in 2016.[10] But small successes like the US Digital Service and 18F signified that more top young talent was going into public service and the government was adapting to attract more. It seemed that progress was heading in the right direction.

And then Donald Trump became president in 2016.

Trump has long been critical of civil servants, accusing "the deep state" of trying to take him down. Trump's rhetoric, coupled with recent budget proposals that would end the public service loan program and freeze income increases for government employees, deterred young people from working in the public sector.[11] In the 2018 federal year, only 28 percent of new hires were under the age of thirty, significantly down from 2016.[12]

As a result of Trump's rhetoric and actions, young people have felt discouraged from government service not only by government outsiders but also by government employees themselves. The State Department lost 12 percent of its foreign-affairs specialists in the first eight months of the Trump

---

10 Danny Vinik, "America's Government is Getting Old," *Politico*, September 27, 2017.

11 Jim Tankersley et al., "Trump's $4.8 Trillion Budget Would Cut Safety Net Programs and Boost Defense," *New York Times*, February 10, 2020.

12 Jeff Neal, "Government Hiring of Young People Continues to Be Terrible," Federal News Network, May 1, 2019.

administration.[13] The number of people who took the foreign service exam in 2019 dropped 22 percent from the previous year.[14] As career foreign-service officers voiced their concerns regarding the calamitous mismanagement of the State Department, young people listened.

How did we get here? How did the situation become so dire?

I've asked this question to hundreds of people—everyone from high-ranking government officials to academics to private sector outsiders. People cite several different reasons: a stifling and frustrating federal bureaucracy, low wages compared to the private sector, and a complex hiring system. But one reason seems to get repeated the most.

"Young people don't think government is cool."

Young people today are characterized as having short attention spans and a desire for immediacy, a product of growing up in the digital era. This conception naturally conflicts with the government, a historically slow-moving beast, which makes the government seem "uncool" and unappealing to an entire generation of young people.

I disagree.

The public sector is highly appealing to Gen Z. In fact, it may be more appealing than to any other generation in history. A

---

13 Jack Corrigan, "The Hollowing-Out of the State Department Continues," *The Atlantic*, February 11, 2018.

14 Dan De Luce, "Fewer Americans Are Opting for Careers at the State Department," *NBC News*, February 25, 2019.

staggering 72 percent of Gen Zers say it's important they have a positive impact in the world. For subsequent generations, that statistic is 68 percent for millennials, 64 percent for Gen Xers, and 63 percent for baby boomers.[15] At its very core, the mission of public service is to do good in the world.

In conducting research for this book, I talked to dozens of young students and professionals in a multitude of sectors. Most of them expressed interest in working in the public sector. They believed in doing service for their country, in doing good, and in being a part of a mission larger than themselves. I was, and still am, completely inspired by the sheer will and determination of my peers.

The issue isn't a lack of demand; young people desperately want to work in the public sector. The government today is simply bogged down by arcane hiring tactics and overly complicated systems that make it nearly impossible for young people to break in. The demand is there, but the barriers to entry are too high. We need to lower them.

So, where did Brandon end up?

In a perfect world, Brandon would have fielded multiple offers from political organizations and go on to a long and illustrious career as a data scientist in the public sector.

But we don't live in a perfect world.

---

15   Caroline Cournoyer, "Generation Z Wants a Job. Are You Ready to Hire Them?" *Governing*, March 23, 2017.

In 2019, Brandon interviewed for data science roles for Super PACs, presidential campaigns, and the Democratic National Committee (DNC). Almost immediately, Brandon started encountering roadblocks in the hiring process.

He landed an interview with a hiring manager for a data director position for Senator Cory Booker's presidential campaign and right away noticed multiple red flags.

"First of all, I had no idea who this guy was; I couldn't find him on LinkedIn. Second, he was probably forty-plus. Third, he didn't have an advanced degree in a technical field."

Compared to the tech hiring process, where hiring managers were typically under thirty-five, had expertly designed LinkedIn profiles, and were heavily credentialed, the government recruitment process seemed paltry.

After the initial interview, Brandon never heard back from the Booker campaign, despite repeated follow-up emails.

This happened time and time again with other campaigns and political organizations.

When interviewing for a technical role at the DNC, the hiring manager was, again, significantly older. Brandon described, "He [sent me] a fifteen-question-long [quiz] with multiple choices and with a bunch of small, repetitive questions. And these things aren't super technical. They're like very surface-level questions and don't dig deep into your [understanding] of technical skills." In addition, "He used a table from 2009. It was 2019 [when I interviewed]. He's using something that's ten years old. Something that's ten years old in start-up time is ancient."

Brandon completed the quiz and sent it back to the DNC. They, too, never responded despite multiple attempts at following up.

Discouraged, Brandon reluctantly returned to the private sector. He now works as a data scientist for a health care tech company.

Brandon had the perfect resume for a governmental hire: technically savvy, bright, and committed to public service. And yet, according to Brandon, the process of recruiting was a terrible experience. He was forced to jump through hoops that made no sense and hiring managers abruptly ghosted him after interviewing. The process of getting a job in the public sector shouldn't be easy; government employees do vital jobs and should be held to the highest standard. However, the process shouldn't be this difficult, this impossible.

Brandon's story—and the stories of thousands like him—is why I decided to write this book.

As I type this, the United States is fighting a pandemic that has disrupted the very way our society operates. The COVID-19 pandemic has proven to be a catalyst for dozens of societal issues—from health care, to immigration, to race relations. The Black Lives Matter movement, which erupted after the murder of George Floyd, is said to be the largest protest movement in the history of the country. At the center of all of this, is Gen Z.

As a college student at the University of Pennsylvania studying philosophy, politics, and economics (PPE), I have always been fascinated with the public sector. I love learning about the origins of our political system, the laws that provide its foundation, and the inner workings of politics. But above all else, I believe in an ideal of service—service to family, service to community, and service to country.

I grew up in a household steeped in the values of business. My parents both studied finance and worked in business. Not a single person in my entire extended family had ever even considered working in the public sector. This was an unknown world. Private sector stalwarts told me stories of government intransigence, dismal pay, and terrible working conditions. I was unsure about a career in public service.

And then I spent a semester in Washington, DC, and everything changed.

In the spring of 2020, I spent a semester in Washington, DC through the Penn in Washington program, taking classes and interning in our country's capital. This was the first time I not only had friends who wanted to go into public service but met people who had spent their careers in government. What struck me the most? People *loved* working for the government. Sure, there were issues of bureaucracy, bad pay, and frustrating practices—everything those private sector advocates had said. But people loved working for a purpose, for a mission larger than themselves. I was completely inspired.

So, I started talking to my friends and peers, telling them about my transformative experience. And surprisingly, many of my peers felt the same way. They were driven to public service and loved the idea of it. But once they tried to break in, they were faced with the beast known as the federal hiring process. There were too many government-specific rules and absurdly long waiting periods. And the private sector made it so much easier. Companies came to campus. They hosted information sessions and brought back recent alumni to pitch the company. They interviewed on campus, extended offers on campus, and hired people within twenty-four hours. There's a pipeline to the private sector but not to the public sector.

Based on all of the abysmal statistics and the dispiriting anecdotes, the future of talent in government seems grim. Despite all of this, I'm relentlessly optimistic. I believe in the next decade we'll see a renaissance in public service for two main reasons.

One, the COVID-19 pandemic has reshaped the political and economic landscape. Faced with the largest recession since 2008, the private sector is extremely unstable. Government positions that offer stable careers and benefits are attractive. But perhaps more consequentially, the pandemic has brought the importance of government to center stage. There are just some things that the private sector can't do and that the public sector must. Now more than ever, the government is essential.

Two, Gen Z is socially committed. Already, this generation has launched social movements and protests relating to everything from climate change to racial justice. As young people grow up and assume positions of power, they will occupy more and more of the public sector.

I call this the *Public Service Renaissance.*

The next decade is poised to shift new talent into the public sector. Gen Zers are motivated and eager to work in the public sector for a purpose larger than themselves. We just have to make government jobs more accessible. Lawmakers, high-level government officials, career public servants, and expert activists must work in tandem to make that possible. The very health of our future government depends on it.

This book will detail the changes government must make in their hiring and recruitment process to facilitate the pivot to the public sector. It's divided into three parts. The first part will focus on how we got here—the history of prestige in government and how business today influences the public sector. The second part will detail how the current hiring system of the government isn't conducive to hiring young people today. Finally, the third part will discuss how to foster the public service pivot and what the government should do to attract young talent.

Throughout the book, you'll read about the stories and experiences of young people and seasoned professionals alike. Those like Hillary Shah, a twenty-year-old first-generation college student committed to social change and public service. Like Clarice Chan, a Presidential Innovation Fellow passionate about the civic tech movement and using tech for good. And like Clare Martorana, a member of the US

Digital Service and the Chief Information Officer for the Office of Personnel Management (OPM), who is determined to bring ten thousand technologists to the government in the next decade.

You'll hear stories of frustration, near hopelessness, and fear. The federal hiring process is a beast like no other; the United States federal government is a beast like no other. But you'll also hear stories of hope—stories that will move you to the very core and inspire you to dream and think higher than you ever thought possible. Because ultimately, the greatest asset of our country is our people—individuals who dare to believe in change when the status quo is intransigence, and individuals who believe the good of our country will prevail above all else.

PART I

HOW DID WE GET HERE?

CHAPTER ONE

BUSINESS INFLUENCE IN THE PUBLIC SECTOR

———

"You know what you should do is go out and make a billion dollars first, and then run for office."

MICHAEL BLOOMBERG.[16]

Michael Bloomberg loves this quote; while I was researching him, a version of this quote came up at least three times. This specific variant comes from a New Yorker profile written in 2009 when Bloomberg was running for his third term as mayor of New York City. The author describes it as a half-joke, but I don't think Bloomberg is joking at all. I think he's completely serious.

Wealthy businesspeople politicians like Michael Bloomberg bring about a complex set of moral dilemmas. How democratic is our society if money can buy overwhelming

---

16   Ben McGrath, "The Untouchable," *The New Yorker*, August 17, 2009.

influence? Does having a lot of money make a politician more or less susceptible to corruption?

This recent influx of businesspeople-turned-politicians has also created a much larger (at least in numbers) issue that will have dire effects on the health of our government and democracy: young people are being told not to start their careers in public service.

> Having Bloomberg and other rich ex-businesspeople in public office sends a message to young people that if they really want to be effective in government, they should go work in business first.

According to a study by the Brookings Institute, 231 congresspeople of the 114th Congress—over 53 percent of the House of Representatives—had previous occupations related to "business or banking."[17] Just fifteen years prior, in the 107th Congress, 159 congresspeople—36 percent of the House—had previous experience in business.[18] The same trend holds true for the Senate; forty-two senators in the 114th Congress have experience in business or banking as compared to twenty-four senators in the 107th Congress. Most other occu-

---

17 Curtlyn Kramer, "Vital Stats: The Growing Influence of Businesspeople in Congress," Brookings Institution, February 17, 2017.

18 Ibid.

pations remained unchanged.[19] Increasingly, it seems that business experience is a prerequisite to a career in politics.

This trend is even more evident in the present day, with both Democrats and Republicans alike.

Besides Michael Bloomberg, who also ran for the Democratic nomination for president in 2020, many other candidates also had extensive business experience. Even among Democrats, who typically try not to flaunt their business experience as much as their Republican counterparts, a substantial number of candidates pointed to their business background as evidence of their governing acumen.

Another billionaire in the Democratic field, Tom Steyer, pointed to his business background as a key differentiating factor between him and his more prominent rivals; "But here's the truth: none of them … have built or run a successful, international business," Steyer said, calling out former Vice President Joe Biden, Massachusetts Senator Elizabeth Warren, Vermont Senator Bernie Sanders, and South Bend, Indiana Mayor Pete Buttigieg by name. "None of them have a private sector track record of creating jobs—none of them have first-hand experience growing wealth and prosperity."[20]

Tech entrepreneur Andrew Yang similarly equated his ability to run a presidential campaign with starting a company. In a tweet from November 2019, Yang wrote, "When people ask if I'm surprised by the success of our campaign, I remind them

---

19 Ibid.
20 Rebecca Klar, "Steyer Touts Business Experience in Economic Address," *The Hill*, December 16, 2019.

that I have founded and run multi-million-dollar organizations that began with just an idea. This feels very familiar. And we are not done yet."[21]

Even the young South Bend mayor, Pete Buttigieg, who at twenty-six-years old already boasted a Harvard degree and a Rhodes scholarship, felt the need to gain business expertise and spent three years at "the firm" (management consulting firm McKinsey). *The New York Times* remarked that Buttigieg's time at McKinsey "set him apart from many of his campaign rivals, underpinning his position as a more centrist alternative to progressive front-runners like Senators Bernie Sanders and Elizabeth Warren."[22]

While recruiting, Buttigieg made it known that he viewed McKinsey as "an asset on the way to a career in public service" rather than a long-term career move. McKinsey not only gave Buttigieg an inside look into corporate America but also credibility as he ran for president a decade later.[23]

Across the aisle, Republican businesspeople brandish their business experience with abandon.

One of the most prominent examples of a Republican businessman turned politician is Mitt Romney. After stints at

---

21 Andrew Yang (@AndrewYang), "When people ask if I'm surprised by the success of our campaign, I remind them that I have founded and run multi-million-dollar organizations that began with just an idea. This feels very familiar. And we are not done yet.," Twitter, November 11, 2019, 2:43 p.m.

22 Michael Forsythe, "When Pete Buttigieg Was One of McKinsey's 'Whiz Kids,'" *New York Times*, December 10, 2019.

23 Ibid.

consulting firms Boston Consulting Group (BCG) and Bain & Company, Romney cofounded private equity firm Bain Capital, a spin-off of the eponymous consulting firm. While running for president in 2012 as the Republican nominee, Romney frequently pointed to his business credentials as proof of his ability to govern; "The lessons I learned over my fifteen years at Bain Capital were valuable in helping me turn around the 2002 Winter Olympics in Salt Lake City. They also helped me as governor of Massachusetts to turn a budget deficit into a surplus and reduce our unemployment rate to 4.7 percent. The lessons from that time would help me as president to fix our economy, create jobs, and get things done in Washington."[24]

Romney went so far as to endorse a constitutional amendment that would require every presidential candidate to have at least three years of business experience: "I was speaking with one of these business owners who owns a couple of restaurants in town. And he said, 'You know I'd like to change the Constitution; I'm not sure I can do it,' he said. 'I'd like to have a provision in the Constitution that in addition to the age of the president and the citizenship of the president and the birthplace of the president being set by the Constitution, I'd like it also to say that the president has to spend at least three years working in business before he could become president of the United States.'"[25]

---

24 Connor Simpson, "Mitt Romney Makes His Bain Defense in *Wall Street Journal* Editorial," *The Atlantic*, August 23, 2012.

25 Catherine Ho, "Romney Suggests Business Experience Should Be Prerequisite to Presidency," *The Washington Post*, June 3, 2012.

Carly Fiorina is another Republican businesswoman who made a foray into politics. After resigning as CEO of technology company Hewlett-Packard (HP) in 2005, Fiorina served as an economic advisor to Senator John McCain during his presidential campaign in 2008. Her following political involvements include running for senator of California in 2010, launching a political action committee (PAC) targeting conservative women, and seeking the Republican Party nomination for president in 2016.[26]

Fiorina positioned herself as a businesswoman rather than a politician and, when running for president, pledged to run the country as a CEO rather than a president. As an ABC News op-ed noted, "[She] talks about governing in terms more akin to a business plan than a policy agenda—placing emphasis on producing measurable results and talking tough about holding bureaucracies accountable, promising a 'top-to-bottom' review of every single agency's budget."[27]

To be clear, business experience itself isn't a negative. Certainly, business expertise does hone skills like leadership, communication, and problem-solving—all relevant to lawmaking and governing. The issue with this recent emphasis on business as a prerequisite to governance is a growing sense that the *only* way to be a good politician, public servant, and leader is to have been in business first. And that notion is dangerous for a functioning democracy. Government, by its very mandate, has a very different purpose than

---

26 "Carly Fiorina Fast Facts," *CNN*, updated June 26, 2020, accessed September 11, 2020.

27 Jordyn Phelps, "How Carly Fiorina Wants to Run the Country Likes a Business," *ABC News*, November 6, 2015.

a private sector company. A private sector business's success is defined, on the most fundamental level, by its profitability. The success of government is defined by different markers: how many people's lives have been improved and how well-ordered is society? It cannot and should not be defined by profitability.

People tend to think anyone can be a politician; most people think they would be better politicians than the ones in office now. But politics and governing are careers just like any other; it requires decades of knowledge and experience to truly master. To be a truly effective political leader, you must have significant institutional knowledge of how government works, how bills are passed, and what decisions to make and when. Businesspeople-turned-politicians like to say their business experiences align with the requirements of politics, but the public sector requires different skills than the private sector. And yet our higher education system, the college-to-company pipeline, and our society of work as a whole fail to make the distinction altogether. It may seem paradoxical, but nowadays, if you're a young person interested in working for the government, it seems more beneficial to go into business first.

***

THE REALITIES OF TODAY

I've seen and experienced the dilemma firsthand. I fell in love with government and law in my Advance Placement US Government and Politics class during my senior year of high school. My teacher, Ms. Warner, assigned my class a month-long mock Supreme Court case. Each one of us played different roles: Supreme Court justices, lawyers, and reporters. I was assigned to play Justice Anthony Kennedy, the swing vote. For a month, I spent hours and hours reading briefing materials, researching the meticulous details of the case, composing insightful questions, and drafting my final opinion. I loved every minute of it. The work was exciting and thrilling, but I grew to appreciate the enormous influence that our government institutions hold over affecting positive change in our country. Even in my mock simulated Supreme Court case, I understood the gravity of public service. I became determined to be a part of that change one day.

And yet, from almost day one at college, I quickly realized that while I met many students eager to make a difference in the world, they weren't pursuing jobs in the public sector. During my freshman year at the University of Pennsylvania, I became familiar with the Penn's pipeline to the finance, consulting, and tech industries. Many of my peers came from families already established in the business world and were determined to utilize their leg up. Most of them weren't necessarily passionate about finance or consulting but wanted the prestige. I heard stories of undecided students seeking guidance from Career Services, which promptly encouraged them to find a job in finance or consulting. The kids who managed to snag internships at investment banks and top-tier consulting firms were revered; it seemed like everyone wanted to be them. They seemed cool.

Finance, consulting, and tech are deemed cool and worthy of an Ivy League education, but working in government isn't. Entrepreneurs and start-ups are deemed revolutionary innovators; public servants are labeled incompetent bureaucrats.

Names like Goldman Sachs, McKinsey, and Bain bring a glint of respect into the eyes of my peers, professors, and potential employers. Clearly, the same effect occurs in politics. Michael Bloomberg, Pete Buttigieg, and Mitt Romney have a level of credibility in large part because of their business backgrounds. As a society, we've placed such a high premium on business expertise and wealth, to the point that we now look for those qualities in our democratic leaders. It's difficult for an aspiring public servant to imagine entering government without those same qualities on their resumes.

These companies have done a phenomenal job capitalizing on young people's desire for concrete business skills. These corporations position themselves as continuations of college, recruiting in classes and providing highly structured mentorship programs for inexperienced college grads. Most firms understand that young grads will likely stay for two years and then leave to explore other opportunities. Finance and consulting corporations market themselves as training grounds for the ambitious-but-undecided twenty-two-year-old.

They make the recruiting process widely accessible to students (at least at top universities), hosting information sessions on campus and virtually, bringing back alumni to campus to pitch to current students, and working closely with each university's career services. And while finance and consulting corporations have a way to go in terms of diversity, most have implemented diversity programs targeting historically underrepresented minorities. From my freshman fall semester, I could tell you the step-by-step consulting and finance recruiting process. After two years as a political science major and spending a semester in Washington DC, I wouldn't even know where to start with the government recruiting process.

Author of *Winners Take All: The Elite Charade of Changing the World*, Anand Giridharadas, described this phenomenon in his book. He succinctly describes how management consulting and finance firms have positioned themselves as premier training grounds for highly motivated young people who want to make a difference in the world. "Management consulting firms and Wall Street financial houses have persuaded many young people in recent years that they provide a superior version of what the liberal arts are said to offer: highly portable training for whatever you wish down the road."[28]

Considering the prevalence of businessmen-turned-politicians today, it's hard to dispute the evidence presented.

Furthermore, these companies know that young people today want to work for a purpose and have marketed themselves as social innovators of good.

In the past ten years, large consulting firms like McKinsey, Bain, and Boston Consulting Group (BCG) have started to heavily increase and highlight their social impact presences.

---

28 Anand Giridharadas, *Winners Take All: The Elite Charade of Changing the World* (New York: Knopf, 2018).

All three have extensive social-sector practices that recruiters heavily emphasize. McKinsey stresses its work with philanthropies, pointing to the fact that they have worked with fifteen of the top twenty-five nonprofits in the United States in the past five years.[29] Bain has pledged to invest $1 billion in pro bono nonprofit consulting over the next ten years.[30] And in 2015, BCG launched the Centre for Public Impact, a nonprofit designed to work with civil servants and change-makers to reimagine government.[31]

On its student recruiting page, consulting firm Deloitte prominently highlighted the value they place in corporate citizenship, the notion that companies have a responsibility to help better society; "We focus on addressing social issues and help drive positive societal change in the communities where we live and work."[32]

Deloitte backs up this claim by encouraging young consultants to work on social impact projects and making pro bono work a part of the culture. According to Ben Mangan, executive director for the Center for Social Sector Leadership at California's Haas School of Business, "Bigger firms like Deloitte and others give full credit to young consultants who work on pro bono projects."[33]

---

29 "Philanthropy," McKinsey, accessed September 04, 2020.
30 "Social Impact," Bain, accessed September 04, 2020.
31 "We Are the Centre for Public Impact," Boston Consulting Group, accessed September 04, 2020.
32 "Top 10 Reasons to Join Deloitte," Deloitte, accessed September 04, 2020.
33 Seb Murray, "Even McKinsey, Bain, BCG Are Offering MBAs Social Impact Consulting Careers," *Business Because,* February 25, 2016.

Even investment banks, which historically have not been seen as bastions of societal good, have pivoted to emphasizing their do-gooder status. Investment bank Morgan Stanley went so far as to state that "having plenty of volunteering opportunities is now one of the big attractions of having a career in banking," citing pro bono initiatives and opportunities to mentor high schoolers.[34] A career in banking is now almost viewed as altruistic in nature.

Do these firms actually do good because of their bleeding hearts or because they're trying to attract top young talent? Idealists will say the former. Cynics will say the latter. I believe it's a little bit of both. Whatever their intentions might be, the private sector is doing an excellent job positioning itself as a driver of social change and attracting top, young talent eager to be a part of that. The public sector isn't. And that's why there's a gap in young government talent today.

34 "For Millennials It's Not Just the Money That Counts," Morgan Stanley, accessed September 04, 2020.

CHAPTER TWO

THE EFFICIENCY PERCEPTION: MILLENNIALS VS. GEN Z

———

Emily Clymer wants to do good with her career, just not in the public sector.

Quick-witted and acerbic, she grew up in the suburbs of Washington DC, shaped by the culture of the federal government. Her indoctrination into politics started young. She debated politics in first grade and went to school with kids from all around the world. Her dad was a lobbyist. Her classmates' dads worked for federal agencies like the State Department and the CIA. The federal government touched almost every aspect of Emily's childhood.

So naturally, she wanted to at least try working in the federal government.

After her freshman year at the University of South Carolina, Emily returned to DC for the summer, looking for an international-facing government internship. After networking with family connections, she managed to secure an internship with the House Committee on Foreign Affairs.

On one hand, it was a fantastic experience. Emily got to organize committee hearings and work with some of the smartest foreign affairs experts in the country. She even got to write a white paper on Cuban repatriation of assets that eventually got incorporated into a bill.

But on the other hand, Emily found the politics of lawmaking frustrating. "You can have a brilliant idea and something that's doing a lot of good in the world, but then someone says, 'I'm not going to vote for that unless you take this part out and put this part in,'" she described. Eventually, "you end up having something brilliant at the beginning until it's very watered down and almost ineffective at the end." The process was long and tedious and not the way she wanted to push for change in the world.

The next summer, Emily networked into a business development role at BAE Systems, a defense contractor that consulted for the federal government. The experience was a stark contrast from her House internship.

"I found at BAE, which is the firm I worked at, that if you have a good idea, you're given a lot of autonomy to run with it. And you have a network of mentors who can help you develop it and shape it, but nothing about your core idea is usually disintegrated," Emily said. The emphasis was on efficiency; "You try to maintain that initial inspiration or goal and basically just utilize many helpful tools and try to get you there as fast and as best as possible." The private sector was naturally more flexible and speedier than the institutional baggage of the public sector.

After graduating from the University of South Carolina in 2018 with a degree in international business, Emily took a job in the private sector as a consultant for IBM, now adamant more than ever to do good through the private sector.

"Growing up in the area, seeing what my dad does as a lobbyist, and then my experience on the Hill and watching those great ideas get watered down, my impression was that you could be a lot more effective for the greater good coming from the private sector. Now, you do have to go through a lot of self-interest in the private sector, but I didn't see how that differs all that much, in reality, from the public sector workers as well. I found that I know that I want to make a difference in the world. I still haven't quite figured out exactly what I want to do, but I think that it's far more likely to happen sooner or happen at all if I'm pushing for that from the private sector."

Emily's perception that the private sector is a more effective driver of social change isn't unique. A common belief among millennials and older American generations is that the government is inefficient and wasteful compared to the private sector. The argument is that the profit-seeking nature of private corporations will naturally lead to cost-cutting and greater customer satisfaction. Therefore, a private sector approach to tackling some of the largest issues facing society is more expedient and appropriate. As I said previously, companies like McKinsey and Goldman Sachs capitalize on this belief and use it to recruit young talent. It's highly effective.

But is the private sector actually more efficient and effective than the public sector? That's a complicated question that could be—and has been—answered with entire books on its own. The short answer seems to be that privatization is less effective than people like to believe. In certain cases, privatization does have a role to play. For example, United States Digital Service modernized Veteran Affairs' (VA) servers by converting the VA's on-premise applications to Amazon Web Services (AWS), all while saving $100 million.[35] This is a prime example of the government and the private sector working together for good.

But in many cases, the public sector is more innovative and effective than the private sector. In her award-winning book, *The Entrepreneurial State*, Professor Mariana Mazzucato debunks the myth that government is entrenched in bureaucracy, showcasing that transformative technologies like the internet, GPS, and touch-screen display were all initially government-funded and researched ventures.[36] So without the government, trillion-dollar industries wouldn't exist today.

---

35   Alan Ning, "Saving VA $100 Million Dollars," *US Digital Service* (blog), April 20, 2018.
36   Mariana Mazzucato, *The Entrepreneurial State: Debunking Public vs. Private Sector Myths* (London: Anthem Press, 2013).

The question I'm asking is how did this very belief—that the private sector is more effective than the public sector—even come to fruition? How has this idea affected the perception of certain careers?

For the better part of the twentieth century, historical circumstances gave the American government an unprecedentedly large mandate. After President Franklin Roosevelt's New Deal and World War II, the American government entered a golden age. The federal government built highways, increased its regulatory authorities, and increased funding for education.

Then, in the 1980s, the winds changed. Business influence didn't get its footing in politics until the Reagan Administration. President Ronald Reagan's ideas of privatization proved to be central in his administration. Increasingly, significant parts of government became privatized, all under the assumption that the private sector would be more effective than the public sector. As he famously ordered, "Don't just stand there, undo something."[37]

In 1987, Reagan created the President's Commission on Privatization, tasked with studying ways government functions could be turned over to private business.[38] This began an

37   John B. Goodman and Gary W. Loveman, "Does Privatization Serve the Public Interest?" *Harvard Business Review*, November-December 1991.

38   Joel Brinkley, "Reagan Appoints Privatization Unit," *New York Times*, September 04, 1987.

onslaught of privatization that has lasted until the present day. In almost every sector—from the military, to health care, to transportation—there exist elements of privatization.

Not only did privatization affect the size and capabilities of government, but it also affected the *perception* of government. We're all affected by society's perception of institutions, whether we want to admit it or not. Millennials grew up in a society marked by the prestige of the private sector over the public sector, never having lived in a pre-Reagan world. It's only natural that millennials believe in the power of the private sector to do good. The privatization of government was simply a fact of their life.

This was all magnified by the digital revolution. When the World Wide Web was created in 1989, its creator, Tim Berners-Lee, hoped that the internet would be used to serve humanity.[39] In the beginning, the internet was the epitome of the utilitarian ideal. Opportunities were endless. Academics and technologists lauded a new era of collaboration that would solve the world's most pressing problems.

And tech companies capitalized on that goodwill. They positioned themselves as arbiters of social good, harnessing the powers of the digital revolution for the public good. Facebook's original mission statement included: "To give people the power to share and make the world more open and connected."[40] Google's original mission was "to organize

---

39   Billy Perrigo, "The World Wide Web Turns 30 Today. Here's How Its Inventor Thinks We Can Fix It," *Time Magazine*, March 12, 2019.

40   Dixie Limbachia, "Mark Zuckerberg Unveils Facebook's New Mission Statement," *Variety*, June 22, 2017.

the world's information and make it universally accessible and useful."[41] The tech industry marketed itself as proprietors of good, creating a culture of do-gooder tech idealists. Millennials bought into it; the glow of tech and the sexiness of entrepreneurship was attractive. Not only did the private sector seem cooler than the government, but it could also accomplish more good than government.

But with Gen Z, the pendulum of power has started to shift back to the public sector.

While the tech sector may have been seen as a bastion of good when millennials were growing up, tech has recently faced a moral reckoning. Issues of antitrust, fake news, online harassment, and privacy concerns all came to light within Gen Z's formative years. While working in the tech industry is still seen as prestigious and sexy, tech's do-gooder badge has been tarnished. Its reputation is no longer clean.

Before the COVID-19 pandemic, the role of government in society seemed to be uncertain. Given increased privatization, Americans were asking themselves, "What role should our institutions serve in our day-to-day lives? What exactly is the importance of government?" The COVID-19 pandemic gave us the answer. Americans were reminded of the essential role government plays in society. From crafting social distancing messaging to coronavirus testing to implementing stimulus packages, there are just some things government must do that the private sector cannot.

---

41   "Our Approach to Search," Google Search, Google, accessed September 07, 2020.

It's too early to tell what far-reaching effect the COVID-19 pandemic will have on the role of government in society moving forward, but I predict government will play a larger role than it did pre-pandemic. The world won't forget this experience any time soon. Certainly, for Gen Z, the COVID-19 pandemic will play a formative role in the shaping of their perception of the public sector. With calamity, the importance of government has been reaffirmed.

Alongside a global pandemic, the United States faced a racial reckoning not seen since the civil rights movement of the 1960s. And Gen Z has been smack-dab in the middle of it all. In a study led by *Business Insider*, nearly 90 percent of Gen Zers believe Black Americans are treated differently than others.[42] In that same study, 77 percent of Gen Zers attended a protest in support of racial equality.[43] Across the country, Gen Zers organized and led protests in hundreds of cities, largely with their social media savvy. In June 2020, seventeen-year-old Simone Jacques led over ten thousand protestors in San Francisco to demand racial justice. And in Washington DC, Gen Zers Kerrigan Williams and Jacqueline LaBayne led a sit-in at the US Capitol, which was largely attended by their peers.[44]

A full seven out of ten Gen Zers believe that the government should do more to solve problems—a figure higher than any

---

42 Dominic Madori-Davis, "The Action Generation: How Gen Z Really Feels about Race, Equality, and Its Role in the Historic George Floyd Protests, Based on a Survey of 39,000 Young Americans," *Business Insider*, June 10, 2020.

43 Ibid.

44 David Gergen and Caroline Cohen, "The Next Greatest Generation," CNN, June 14, 2020.

other generation in the United States.[45] Young people believe that true systemic change comes through our basic institutions and requires policy input. The COVID-19 pandemic and the Black Lives Matter movement are the two most transformative events of this generation, forever altering the way we perceive our government and its role in society. All of this points to a renaissance in public service.

How do Gen Z and the social movements of today compare to past generations, namely baby boomers and the watershed events of the 1960s? In some ways, the generations are very similar. At their very peak, the baby boomers represented 37 percent of the United States population, providing the bulk of protestors in the sixties.[46] Similarly, Gen Z has been an integral part of protests of the last five years. According to a poll released by the Kaiser Family Foundation, young people ages eighteen to twenty-nine account for 52 percent of all adults who have protested—double the share of their portion of the overall population.[47]

Yet based on early indicators, the impact of Gen Z and baby boomers on politics and government seem to differ in one critical way. While baby boomers transformed American society culturally, they ultimately failed to succeed electorally. Conservative presidents (besides Jimmy Carter), who positioned themselves against the cultural changes of the

45   Kim Parker and Ruth Igielnik, "On the Cusp of Adulthood and Facing an Uncertain Future: What We Know About Gen Z So Far," Pew Research Center, May 14, 2020.

46   Ronald Brownstein, "The Race Unifying Boomers and Gen Z," *The Atlantic*, June 18, 2020.

47   Ibid.

sixties, dominated the political sphere until Bill Clinton was elected in 1992.[48] And while Gen Zers are just starting to become of voting age, they already wield substantial political power.

Nationwide, 61 percent of eighteen to twenty-nine-year-olds voted for President Joe Biden, with young voters of color overwhelmingly casting ballots for him.[49] According to analysis from the Center for Information & Research on Civic Learning and Engagement (CIRCLE), youth voters favored Biden over Trump by a margin of more than one hundred thousand votes each in swing states like Arizona, Michigan, Georgia, and Pennsylvania—a significant chunk of Biden's margin of victory.[50] While most of Gen Z has yet to reach voting age, the 2020 election is early proof that Gen Z may be politically more influential than its boomer predecessor.

Of course, civic engagement doesn't necessarily translate to increased public service. Especially given the current political climate, predicting a rise in public service from Gen Zers might seem paradoxical. Trust in institutions is at an all-time low; just 19 percent of Gen Zers believe the US is heading in the right direction, a 12 percent decrease due to the COVID pandemic and the Black Lives Matter movement.[51] How does this bode well for the future?

---

48 Ibid.
49 Angela Nelson, "Young Voters Were Crucial to Biden's Win," *TuftsNow*, November 12, 2020.
50 Ibid.
51 Nick Laughlin, "How 2020 is Impacting Gen Z's Worldview," *Morning Consult*, July 6, 2020.

While Gen Z is less optimistic about the future, they increasingly believe they can shape it. And 62 percent of Gen Zers believe they have the potential to impact the world.[52] While Gen Z may not trust government institutions now, they strongly believe they can change government for the better. Our generation has reached a tipping point. Frustration has boiled over into a desire for change. In other words, Gen Z doesn't have faith in what government is today but what government *could* be in the future.

One of those Gen Zers is Hillary Shah, a rising senior studying political science and economics at the University of North Texas. Hillary—who was recently named a finalist for the prestigious Truman Scholarship, which recognizes students dedicated to public service—has been committed to social activism and political change since high school. At just twenty years old, she has founded a youth political engagement organization in her hometown, served as vice president of the Student Body at the University of North Texas, and recently completed an internship with the Civil Rights Division of the Department of Commerce. She told me that public service is the only career she has ever seriously considered.

In addition, Hillary is part of a generation of young women determined to speak out about injustice. From Greta Thunberg fighting for climate change awareness, to Malala Yousafzai advocating for girl's education, to Emma Gonzalez protesting for gun control, this generation of female activists is poised to affect public discourse in new and consequential ways.

---

52 Ibid.

Hillary speaks about government in blunt terms. When I asked her about Gen Z and public service, Hillary was unapologetic; "I think our generation especially has been through so much—two recessions, so much documented racial injustice. We have been betrayed by our government in a more blatantly transparent way than past generations, so I think we are more likely to go into activism or public service."

Hillary's unforgiving description of the government struck a chord with me. I could relate to her anger and disappointment with our government. My peers and I have lived in a post-9/11 world, seemingly going from one disaster to another: two wars, two recessions, an environmental crisis, gun violence, a pandemic, and severe racial injustice. Depression and anxiety rates among young people have shot through the roof. Suicide rates have doubled for girls and young women between 2000 and 2017.[53] In 2017, boys and young men ages fifteen to nineteen committed suicide at a rate of 17.9 per one hundred thousand, an increase from 13 per one hundred thousand in 2000.[54] At times, the future sometimes seems overwhelmingly bleak.

So I asked Hillary something I didn't plan on asking. I asked her how she stayed motivated to fight for change despite the obstacles in her way. Why did she care so much?

Hillary told me a story about the first protest she organized. She grew up in Frisco, Texas, a very white, very conservative suburb. As a first-generation daughter of Indian immigrants,

---

53   Emily Seymour, "Gen Z: Studies Show Higher Rates of Depression," VOA News, August 25, 2019.

54   Ibid.

public service felt almost like a calling. She felt it was her duty to advocate for underrepresented voices in her community and to fight against injustice. It felt weird not to care.

In the wake of the 2018 Parkland shooting that killed seventeen people, Hillary organized a district-wide school walkout in protest of gun violence. A staggering 2500 students participated in the walkout. Yet, there was a massive amount of backlash against the protest, largely from gun rights activists.

"My friends and I literally thought we were going to die. We got death threats; people showed up to school with AK-47s. My friend and I—who were both women of color—were told to go back to Mexico. I was terrified."

But the backlash didn't deter her. In fact, it strengthened her resolve.

"My first reaction to the backlash of the protests was fear. But my second reaction right after was, 'Why do people care? It's just a bunch of teenagers doing this; why does it matter so much?' And I came to the conclusion that it was because my voice really mattered, and it was because I was doing something unprecedented that could make an impact. And people don't want impact."

To me, that sums up the Gen Z mentality: resilience in the face of resistance, determination despite obstacles. A desire for change, driven by a deep understanding of the consequences if society doesn't change. And despite all the cynicism, enduring optimism for what government can do and could be.

PART II

WHAT ARE THE PROBLEMS WITH THE SYSTEM NOW?

CHAPTER THREE

ISSUES WITH THE PUBLIC SECTOR TALENT PIPELINE

———

Judge Lydia Griggsby has had one of the most distinguished careers in public service, spanning twenty-plus years and within several different areas of the federal government. Yet as a student, she couldn't imagine it ever happening.

As a political science major at the University of Pennsylvania, Judge Griggsby knew she was interested in government and the public sector, yet there were no programs or resources to help her navigate her options in the public sector. Career services emphasized private sector opportunities in finance and consulting. As she described to me, "I found as a student, it was really hard to learn about other paths that aren't the big firm path, like government or public interest, things of that nature."

Learning about career paths that weren't mainstream on campus seemed unnecessarily difficult.

After graduating, Judge Griggsby went straight to law school at Georgetown. And yet, despite going to school in the heart of the federal government, Judge Griggsby found that law school wasn't much better than undergrad in detailing potential careers in the public sector.

"I didn't even know about opportunities as a young lawyer that didn't involve going into a law firm and kind of getting on that track. We were all doing it; that was kind of just understood as a standard at that time at Georgetown."

Joining a big, private law firm right out of law school was expected of law students. It was simply the norm among her classmates and peers.

So that's what she did. After graduating from Georgetown, Judge Griggsby headed to DLA Piper, one of the largest and most prestigious law firms in the country. A lot was worthwhile about the experience. She connected with experienced lawyers, gained valuable training, and learned about the business of law firms. But the work was simply not what she wanted to do.

"I had little interest substantively in what I was doing. As a junior associate, you kind of get placed where you get placed. I did commercial real estate legal work. But for me, it just wasn't a practice area that I particularly found interesting or stimulating. It wasn't something that I said, 'Yeah, I'm going to do this for the next fifteen years of my professional life.'"

As she considered her next move, Judge Griggsby had a vague idea that she wanted to return to Washington DC and work in government. On a lark, she applied to the Department of Justice (DOJ), a notoriously difficult agency to break into because of the prestige it holds in the legal community, hoping that she would get in someday three or four years down the road. Miraculously, despite not having a single connection in the DOJ, she was hired as a trial attorney in the Commercial Litigation Branch of the Civil Division of the DOJ.

Immediately, Judge Griggsby fell in love with government and the responsibility of the work.

"It offered me a much bigger world, coming to work at the Justice Department, the biggest law firm in the world. Representing the United States government was a huge deal to me, and being really young and given the level of responsibility that you get in the public sector, you can't match that."

Judge Griggsby's career skyrocketed to extraordinary heights in the public sector. After serving as a trial attorney at DOJ, she served as an Assistant United States Attorney in the District of Columbia. Judge Griggsby then jumped to a different branch of government—Congress—working as Counsel for the United States Select Committee on Ethics and the Chief Counsel for Privacy and Information Policy for the United States Senate Committee on the Judiciary.

Finally, in 2014, President Obama nominated Judge Griggsby to serve as a judge on the United States Court of Federal Claims. She was subsequently confirmed and has now served as a federal judge for over six years.

"I'm now a judge at the court that I first litigated before as a twenty-seven, twenty-eight-year-old lawyer, where I first stood up in court and said my name and the phrase, 'I'm representing the United States of America.' Ultimately, working in public service wasn't so much a career strategy for me. I followed my heart and really thought about what I wanted to do. And I knew the kind of work I wanted to do was in the government in Washington, DC."

From indecisive law student to federal judge, Judge Griggsby has certainly had an extraordinarily distinguished career in public service. This is the success story. And yet, every year, thousands of immensely qualified, passionate students, with Judge Griggsby's potential, never even get the chance to enter public service, simply because they're unaware of the opportunities. There's no pipeline, no clear pathway to follow into the public sector out of school.

Think of all the Judge Griggsbys we could have in the federal government if there was a school to public service pipeline.

***

PROBLEMS WITH GOVERNMENT RECRUITING TODAY

So what's wrong with government recruiting today? Why can't it attract top talent?

It's not due to a lack of interest. According to a report by the Partnership for Public Service and the National Association of Colleges and Employers, 24.9 percent of college students ranked government (federal, state, and local) as one of their top three target industries. Among graduating seniors, government was the highest-ranked industry, yet only 2 percent of students surveyed planned to enter federal service after graduation.[55]

Simply put, the pipeline isn't there. Whereas private sector companies have spent the last few decades cultivating substantial talent pipelines, public sector agencies have failed to do so. This has led to a major shortage of talent and future leaders in government as the private sector becomes increasingly popular to students. To understand where government's recruiting shortcomings lie and how it can be enhanced to attract Gen Z talent, we must compare private sector talent pipelines to the public sector's recruiting tactics today.

According to a recent study conducted by Monster and research firm Market Connections, HR professionals in the private sector are twice as likely to use social media and digital platforms to recruit compared to their public sector HR counterparts.[56] Only 35 percent of federal agencies use social media sites and commercial job ads to find talent, while 75 percent depend on USAJobs—the notoriously onerous and unnecessarily complicated government job board—to fill vacancies.[57]

---

55 *College Students Are Attracted to Federal Service, but Agencies Need to Capitalize on Their Interest* (Washington DC: Partnership for Public Service and National Association of College and Employees, 2014).

56 Susan Fallon Brown, "Four Traps in Federal Recruiting, and How to Avoid Them," *Government Executive*, October 31, 2018.

57 Ibid.

Why does this matter? Gen Zers are digital natives and are more tech savvy than any other generation. A vast majority of them only look for job opportunities online. Factoring this notion in, a whopping 65 percent of federal agencies are missing out on an entire crop of Gen Z talent. In addition, too many government agencies still use paper in their hiring process.[58] This is an immediate turnoff to most Gen Z candidates. Almost everything nowadays gets done digitally, whether it be online classes, digital contracts, or direct deposit payments. Applying for a position on physical paper seems archaic.

Conversely, private sector companies have long utilized social media and online job boards to attract young talent. Campus recruiters for companies have cultivated strong social media profiles on platforms like LinkedIn, Instagram, and Facebook as well as bought targeted ads regarding upcoming information sessions at specific schools. Recruiters will post openings on job boards like Handshake, a college-specific job recruiting board. But campus recruiters don't simply post openings and wait for students to start to apply; recruiters will individually message potential candidates, offering individualized attention, which appeals to Gen Zers. Individually messaging candidates is the extra step that students will take note of as they start looking for internships and jobs.

When it comes to the initial application process, the first step in applying for private sector companies is almost always easily accessible and digital. For example, consulting firms and

---

58   Anna Peters, "Recruitment Strategies for Government Agencies to Quickly Hire Students and Grads at Scale," *College Recruiter*, March 29, 2018.

investment banks will allow for applicants to apply in less than five minutes, requiring simply a resume and transcript. Not only does this allow for the greatest number of applications for openings, but it allows corporations to do an easy screening of applicants, weeding out unqualified candidates before proceeding to interviews.

But in government, that first step is unnecessarily difficult. The federal government's job board, USAJobs, is universally disliked by job hunters in the public sector. In fact, in Washington DC—a town notoriously known for its gridlock and partisanship—hatred of USAJobs may be the one sentiment universally shared by individuals of all different political viewpoints. Not only does the site require a "federal resume" that differs from the standard private sector resume, but some applications take over an hour to complete—not ideal for students leading busy college lives.

Private sector firms also make an appearance at campus career fairs, but for most companies, that's just the tip of the recruiting iceberg. Private sector recruiters make an effort to build relationships with each university's career services center. Career services can serve as a gatekeeper to top talent. Companies with the best relationships with career services are allowed inside access to top talent as they are seen as trustworthy and popular destinations for students post-graduation.

Most government agencies that do visit campus simply attend generic campus college fairs and fail to personalize their recruiting outreach. For example, I only see government recruiters once a year at the annual public sector career fair.

Even then, only a few agencies and local government departments make an effort to show up and interact with students.

In addition, private sector companies also host information sessions early in the recruiting season to attract top talent early on. Those information sessions are designed to impress. For example, at the University of Pennsylvania, Bain, a prestigious management consulting firm, hosted an information session last fall at the beginning of the school year for over a thousand students. In attendance were recruiters, but also partners, mid-level associates, and thirty students who had recently completed summer internships. While having partners present is a major draw for students, having young alums returning to campus to talk about their current jobs really influences students. Those alums serve as perfect conduits for companies to attract and explain what it's like to work for that specific organization.

Private sector corporations also get creative with their recruiting. Oftentimes, companies will sponsor club events or competitions for students. For example, the consulting firm Accenture sponsors a case competition for students every year, allowing students to develop consulting skills while simultaneously recruiting talent early. Other companies, like the investment bank Morgan Stanley, will sponsor finance club events to heighten name recognition and target specific populations on campus.

It's not that government doesn't have opportunities available for recent college graduates; programs like the Pathways Programs, the Workforce Recruitment Program, and the Presidential Management Fellows Program are all designed to specifically attract and cultivate young talent. However, the public sector does a poor job in marketing opportunities to students. The demand is there and the opportunities are there; we just need to connect the two.

***

DIVERSITY OR THE LACK THEREOF

For minority students and young professionals, quality government opportunities are even harder to find. When diversity in the federal government is looked at holistically, it might seem that government doesn't have a diversity issue. According to the Office of Personnel Management (OPM), minorities comprise 38 percent of the federal workforce, roughly equivalent to the percentage of minorities in the US population.[59] However, while minorities comprise 38 percent of the federal workforce, they make up just 22 percent of senior leadership roles.[60] Clearly, the public sector still has a major diversity issue.

Tinisha Agramonte would know. As the former director of the Office of Civil Rights at the Department of Commerce, Tinisha was one of the few African American females to serve at the highest levels of government. But her long and illustrious career in public service happened by complete accident.

As a first-generation, low-income student at California State University-Hayward, Tinisha had no idea how to pursue

---

59 Dan Durak and Wendy Ginsberg, "Government's Lack of Diversity in Leadership Positions," *Partnership for Public Service*, March 11, 2019.
60 Ibid.

a professional career. Getting into college was a major goal in itself. Her family viewed college as the end goal, but no one, including Tinisha herself, understood how to navigate college life and post-graduation life. As she struggled to balance three jobs while attending school full time, pursuing a professional career seemed almost impossible, much less one in the public sector.

When Tinisha moved to the United Kingdom with her husband who was in the US military, she realized that she could work for the government. "I saw all these people wearing normal clothes around the military base and asked my husband, 'Hey, who are those people who work in government in regular clothes?' My husband responded, 'Oh, they're civilians.'" Tinisha had no idea civilians could work for the government. Government recruiters didn't come to her school; the public sector wasn't remotely on her radar.

Immediately, Tinisha was intrigued. Government work seemed interesting and meaningful, but, above all else, it seemed stable and convenient. This wasn't the most aspirational reason, but it was a highly powerful reason, nonetheless. For a first-generation professional like herself, stability was a golden ticket. She had stumbled into a career she didn't know existed.

Tinisha got a job in the Department of Veterans Affairs, and her career shot upward from there. Tinisha rose to become the director of Outreach and Retention at the Department of Veteran Affairs. Then, she took a position as the assistant administrator for the Office of Diversity, Inclusion and Civil Rights at the US Small Business Administration. Finally, in

2015, Tinisha became the director of the Office of Civil Rights for the US Department of Commerce, where she launched the First-Generation Professionals Initiative, a program designed to support first-generation federal government professionals. For over fifteen years, Tinisha's impact in the federal government has been widespread and substantial. And it almost didn't happen.

Tinisha, like many people, stumbled into working for the government. But the public sector can't afford to only attract talent by pure happenstance. For every individual that stumbles into public service and succeeds, there are ten more that could have succeeded but didn't know public service was even an option. Attracting diverse talent shouldn't be a matter of chance. That's why a diverse talent pipeline is critical to the success and effectiveness of the government.

While diversity recruitment has made substantial progress in the past few decades, there's still a way to go. Government should expand its recruiting efforts to target Historically Black Colleges and Universities (HBCUs) and Hispanic-serving institutions, as well as community colleges and state schools. Oftentimes, students at overlooked universities struggle with gaining access to certain industries because of a lack of alumni networks.

Take Hillary Shah, the rising senior at the University of North Texas committed to a career in public service, for example. Hillary described having to work twice as hard as her internship peers from elite universities to get her internship in the federal government; "All of my peers that I have met at UNT [University of North Texas] are just as smart, if not smarter, than the peers that I had at the Department of Commerce. They just didn't know that they were capable of having these opportunities."

Hillary advocates for government recruiters to make a specialized effort to recruit from diverse populations at state schools and community colleges. "It would make such an impact if the federal government cared enough to reach out to us."

There are so many recruiting gimmicks out there—branded reusable straws, witty social media posts, free pizza. But ultimately, none of that matters unless organizations are being authentic and genuinely interested in attracting quality candidates. At the end of the day, students just want to feel like they're being seen.

THREE ACTIONS THE FEDERAL GOVERNMENT SHOULD TAKE TO IMPROVE THE PUBLIC SECTOR TALENT PIPELINE:

1. Agency recruiters should focus on making personalized connections with potential Gen Z hires. This can be done through establishing relationships with certain university career centers, reaching out to candidates through social media outlets like LinkedIn and Twitter, and connecting with relevant student organizations on campus like College Democrats, College Republicans, nonpartisan political groups, and other industry-specific organizations. (Note, I will discuss this in more detail in Chapter 6.)

2. The Office of Personnel Management (OPM) and HR departments at specific agencies must digitize and sim-

plify the application process. USAJobs should be stream-lined, redesigned to be more user-friendly, and should allow applicants to use their normal resumes instead of the federal resume. The initial application should be shortened, allowing applicants to apply more easily.

3. Increasing outreach to underrepresented communities is essential. Government agencies should make an effort to connect with career centers at HBCUs as well as universities in rural areas. Agencies should also recruit current employees of underrepresented backgrounds to go to campuses and help in diversity recruitment efforts.

CHAPTER 4

ISSUES WITH THE FEDERAL HIRING PROCESS

———

How long would you wait to hear if you've been accepted for a position? A month? Six months? Would you wait two and a half years? Probably not. You'd move on to other opportunities. And yet, that's how long Amy had to wait to break into public service.[61]

Amy was one of the kids who had her entire career path mapped out. She studied international relations and Arabic in college and had studied abroad in the Middle East. She was set on joining the State Department as a Foreign Service officer.

But that's not how her career turned out. Right after college, Amy spent a year as a Fulbright scholar, living in a rural

---

61   Pseudonym at the request of interviewee.

community with limited internet connectivity. While she loved her experience, she realized she wanted to be based in the United States and decided to put off the Foreign Service. When Amy returned home, she got a job at a global health company. There she became interested in the public health aspect of global health work. She decided to apply to graduate school and study public health, intent on getting a public health position in the federal government after graduating.

While at grad school, Amy accepted an internship at the Center for Disease Control (CDC) focusing on environmental health. There, she first learned about the United States Public Health Service Commissioned Corps (USPHS).

"While there [at the CDC], there were all these people in khaki uniforms walking around, and I asked myself, 'Why on earth is the navy here in Atlanta at the CDC?' Of course, as I shortly learned, it was the US Public Health Service, not the navy."

USPHS is one of the eight uniformed military services of the United States and is charged with protecting and advancing the nation's health. Their ranks include doctors, nurses, engineers, environmental health specialists, scientists, and other health professionals. Its officers have been deployed in response to multiple crises, including 9/11, Hurricane Sandy, the Ebola outbreak, and the COVID-19 pandemic, among many others.

During her time at the CDC, Amy became more and more certain that she wanted to join the Public Health Service: "I just instantly wanted to be a part of this community. They were just the best people in the room. They went out of their way to be excellent at their job and to be mentors to me. They were just fabulous."

In her last year of grad school, Amy applied to the Public Health Service. While waiting to hear back, Amy continued to apply for public health positions in both the public and private sectors. She had mentors who had warned her that the Corps took a while to vet and accept candidates. They always warned her not to quit her day job.

So in February of her final year of grad school, Amy accepted a fellowship offer from another federal agency. To Amy, the next few years looked set. "I was like, 'This is great. I'm going to a new city and complete this fellowship. Then I'll enter the Public Health Service.'" It was a perfect plan.

But by June, the federal agency was still not ready for Amy to start the onboarding process. So, she took some time to travel, spending a few months in Canada working on forest management and other random odd jobs that had always been on her bucket list.

But when she returned to the United States in October and the agency still couldn't give her a start date, Amy started to get a bit worried. "Working through their hiring process I was like, 'Well, I don't have health insurance.' I had quit my other job in anticipation of this fellowship starting. I was a little bit nervous." Amy couldn't wait forever. She had rent to pay, groceries to buy, and no health insurance. As much as she loved the offer from the fellowship, she had to turn it down.

Eventually, after 180 USAJobs applications and six responses, Amy managed to land a position with a different federal agency as a health scientist. Shortly afterward, Amy was finally accepted into the Public Health Service. Within the waiting period, she had completed a year of graduate school, gone through two separate extensive job searches, and worked multiple jobs in two different countries. The federal hiring process is, categorically, an absurdly long and tedious undertaking that only a few ultimately make it through.

Now, two years into her service as an officer in the Public Health Service, Amy loves her job. The work can be tiring, stressful, and travel-intensive but also incredibly rewarding and meaningful. Just from talking to Amy, I could tell how much she valued her work. I interviewed Amy as she was deploying to rural Texas in response to the COVID-19 pandemic. In our hour-long conversation, not once did I hear a complaint or a grievance. Instead, I heard the opposite; she said she felt honored and incredibly grateful to be of service to underserved communities and the country in a time of need. We need more people like Amy in the federal government—people who are committed, determined, and passionate about the greater good.

Even for people already interested in working for the government, the federal onboarding process is too long and complicated for many to stick through the entire process. Amy managed to break into government service thanks to relentless patience. But she shouldn't have had to wait two-and-a-half years to do so. No one should.

We've talked about the issues the government has in developing a talent pipeline, but what about the issues facing young, motivated people who have already applied for government positions? When considering the problem of a lack of young talent in public service, most pundits and government officials look to how government can better attract young people. And while that's certainly part of the equation, another key part that often gets ignored is how the government hiring process fails to convert demonstrated interest into full-time positions. Why is the federal hiring process so complex and lengthy? And how does the government hiring process disproportionately negatively affect young people?

To examine the issues of the federal hiring process, we must first understand the process altogether. In summary, it's a lengthy and intricate ten-step process:

1. **Posting Closes** → Once you submit your application (usually through the US government's job application system, USAJobs), you must wait for the job posting to close before you hear back. Government agencies are strict on closing dates and rarely accept late applications.

2. **Screening of Applications** → Government human resources departments are relentlessly strict with minimum requirements and are notoriously inflexible. HR specialists will sort through all their applications and eliminate any applicants that don't meet the minimum requirements. It's important to note here that most federal positions don't accept traditional private sector resumes but require the creation of a federal resume. The main difference between a private sector resume and a federal resume is that a federal resume is much more detailed.

An ideal federal resume should feature the last ten years of employment history and sometimes requires a separate knowledge, skills, and abilities statement. Altogether, a federal resume is between three to five pages.[62]

3. **Finalist List** → The HR department and the hiring manager work to create a short list of finalists exclusively based on information included in the applications and on the federal resume.

4. **Interviews Are Scheduled** → The hiring manager will call finalists for an interview.

5. **Background and Reference Checks** → Many sectors of government conduct background and reference checks at this stage; however, some organizations wait until they're ready to make an offer to save money.

6. **Interviews Are Conducted** → The finalists are interviewed, which can take anywhere from one week to months.

7. **Selection of New Hire** → After all the finalists have been interviewed, the interviewer or interview panel decides which finalist will get the position and rank the other finalists.

8. **Job Offer is Extended** → A verbal job offer is extended so salary and start date negotiations can begin.

9. **Job Offer is Accepted** → The chosen finalist formally accepts the job offer in writing so the paperwork process can begin. It's important to note that many government departments require security clearances, which can result in a lengthy waiting period. The security process can take anywhere from two weeks to one year, with the average length being around three months.

---

62 "How to Build a Federal Resume (With Template)," Career Guide, Indeed, accessed September 11, 2020.

10. **Candidates Not Selected Are Notified (or not)** → Once the organization and the chosen finalist have agreed upon the terms, the organization notifies all other applicants (not just finalists, but every original applicant) that the position is filled. However, some government departments fail to notify applicants at all of a filled position.

Altogether, the general federal hiring process, from application to first day on the job, can take anywhere from three months to over a year.[63]

In addition, the very structure of the federal hiring process disadvantages younger applicants. Applicants for federal government positions are grouped into three categories: competitive appointments, noncompetitive appointments, and excepted service.

Noncompetitive appointments and excepted service individuals receive the most streamlined federal hiring process. Noncompetitive appointments consist of federal employees who have been in the federal government for at least three years. Under this authority, hiring managers may hire individuals without going through the entire lengthy hiring process. Noncompetitive status rewards government employment and provides an incentive for continued public service, an objectively positive goal.

Nevertheless, it disproportionately affects young people looking to break into the public sector. In fact, a significant

---

63 Michael Roberts, "10 Steps in the Government Hiring Process," *The Balance Careers*, June 25, 2019.

portion of openings posted to USAJobs is already filled by existing federal employees, limiting the number of openings for young graduates who don't possess government work experience. A report done by the US Merit Systems Protection Board states that "66 percent of HR staff reported that vacancies were advertised to all Federal employees all or most of the time," compared to just 48 percent of HR staff reporting that vacancies were advertised to all sources—including nonfederal employees—all or most of the time.[64]

Excepted service applicants include hard-to-recruit positions like medical doctors and attorneys. The argument here is that a streamlined hiring process could help attract hard-to-fill positions that require graduate and professional degrees and specific skill sets. This is again, without a doubt, an objectively positive goal. The federal government needs highly qualified, talented professionals to effectively serve American society. And yet, the ranks of the excepted service candidates rarely account for young people simply because they haven't yet completed higher levels of professional training and gained the prerequisite experience.

Therefore, most young people looking to work for the federal government theoretically fall into the competitive appointments category. Competitive status includes all individuals who don't register for noncompetitive or excepted service status, not qualifying for a streamlined federal hiring process. All competitive status applicants must go through the full,

---

64 Susan Tsui Grindmann, "The Impact of Recruitment Strategy on Fair and Open Competition for Federal Jobs," *A Report to the President and the Congress of the United States by the US Merit Systems Protection Board* (Washington, DC: US Merit Systems Protection Board, 2015).

ten-step hiring process. For young professionals and recent college graduates, the extensive process is untenable.

The federal government isn't oblivious to the issues. In the past thirty years, the government has launched several programs targeting young people, hoping to solidify the future workforce. These efforts have resulted in the Pathways Program, which provides structured internship programs and post-graduation opportunities across the federal government; the Presidential Management Fellows (PMF) Program, a highly selective rotational program for advanced degree candidates; and the Workforce Recruitment Program, which matches students in higher education who have varying degrees of physical and mental disabilities to federal jobs.[65]

These programs have all streamlined hiring procedures and recruit young people specifically. And in many respects, the programs worked. According to one Pathways participant, almost all the young professionals she knows working in the federal government came through one of the designated programs. Yet those programs have limited capacity. The number of program participants doesn't nearly account for the number of young people in the federal workforce required to ensure a stable government talent pipeline. Furthermore, even with the streamlined hiring processes, going through one of these programs still requires months of interviewing and onboarding, much longer than the private sector.

---

65 "Policy, Data, Oversight," Hiring Information, OPM, accessed September 18, 2020.

Sophie would know.[66] She was one of the rare twenty-four-year-olds who managed to break into the public sector right out of college. But the process was still incredibly challenging.

After completing a congressional internship on the Hill her junior year, Sophie was determined to return to Washington DC. After graduating with a business degree in 2018, she went searching for jobs in the federal government. A friend recommended the Workforce Recruitment Program, and Sophie was sold.

Sophie immediately applied and was matched with a recruiter from the Department of Labor. Because she was in the Workforce Recruitment Program, the hiring process was supposed to be easier and more streamlined. But the federal hiring process in general is a total beast of its own kind. Going through the federal hiring process through the Workforce Recruitment Program is a little easier, but still complicated and lengthy.

As Sophie noted, the Workforce Recruitment Program eases the process to an extent; "You get to submit your own resume that can look like the private sector version. And if they want to hire you, they can hire you and onboard you on the spot." This effectively eliminates steps three to seven of the general federal hiring process.

Yet the streamlined process wasn't without its challenges. "It still takes a very long time. You have to work out security clearances and the general paperwork, and for whatever

---

66 Pseudonym at the request of interviewee.

reason, it's just so slow moving. It's like 90 to 120 days is the average range of getting someone hired and onboarded. It's crazy."

A ninety-day turnaround isn't feasible for many recent college graduates. A twenty-two-year-old graduating with $100,000 in student debt can't afford to wait ninety days to receive a paycheck. They have to pay their student loans. A twenty-two-year-old living in California can't wait ninety days to relocate across the country. They have to find a place to live.

When tech companies like Google and Facebook hire students within weeks (or days) and offer generous relocation packages, it's hard for government to compete.

THREE ACTIONS THE FEDERAL GOVERNMENT SHOULD TAKE TO IMPROVE THE FEDERAL HIRING PROCESS:

1. Fix USAJobs! This will come up multiple times throughout the book because USAJobs is just that annoying and frustrating to everyone. USAJobs has been called a "black hole" for applicants, with up to 50 percent of jobs posted on the website going without a selection.[67] USAJobs must be condensed and streamlined for a better user experience, and applications must be shortened to reduce selection and onboarding time. More on this in Chapter 7.
2. The government should reduce interview periods. Interviews with candidates should take place within two weeks to better compare candidates and send offers out quicker.

---

67   Dave Nyczepir, "USDS Wants to Fix the 'Black Hole; USAJOBS With Alternative Hiring Assessment," *FedScoop*, October 23, 2019.

3. Move the recruiting timeline from the spring to the fall/ winter. Most private sector recruiting timelines happen in September/October, whereas the public sector doesn't even start to interview applicants until March/April. This awkward gap forces students who want to work in government to instead commit to a private sector job out of fear of not getting a job whatsoever. Moving the recruiting timeline up would allow students to actively pursue public sector options alongside private sector ones.

CHAPTER FIVE

GOVERNMENT PAY

———

Let's talk about money.

The general consensus in society is that government pays less than the private sector. People commonly cite pay as one of the largest reasons government fails to attract talent, but is that conception true? In short—sort of.

According to a report by the Congressional Budget Office, federal citizen workers with a bachelor's degree earn approximately 5 percent more than their private sector counterparts when considering wages and benefits.[68] Even federal workers with master's degrees earn slightly more than private sector peers with the same level of education. However, the real discrepancy between public and private sector compensation lies with individuals who have professional or doctorate degrees. Private sector professionals with advanced degrees

---

68 "Comparing the Compensation of Federal and Private sector Employees, 2011 to 2015," Report (Washington, DC: Congressional Budget Office, 2017).

earn 24 percent more in wages and benefits than public sector professionals.[69]

Clearly, the wide gap in compensation between the public and private sector at the highest levels of education hinders government's ability to attract top talent away from the private sector. However, not only does the discrepancy affect already established professionals, but it also negatively influences young, highly motivated individuals as well. Young college students and recent graduates look to future compensation as an indicator of growth opportunities. This large divide between individuals with professional degrees serves as a deterrent.

Let's look at a subsection of the federal workforce that's chronically underpaid and almost entirely made up of young people: government internships. The federal government has long been criticized for not paying or underpaying its interns. According to the nonprofit Pay Our Interns, 61 percent of congressional representatives don't pay their interns.[70] This creates a system where minorities and low-income students are shut out from government opportunities, leading to a major representation issue in the federal government. If only the rich (and therefore, predominantly white students) can afford to work in the public sector, government will subsequently reflect that.

---

69   Ibid.
70   James R. Jones, "The Color of Congress: Racial Representation Among Interns in the US House of Representatives," Report (Washington, DC: Pay Our Interns, 2016).

When Hillary Shah received an internship offer from the Department of Commerce's Civil Rights office, she was thrilled. She loved the people she had met while interviewing for the position, and the internship allowed her to help create professional opportunities for other first-generation, low-income students like herself. It was a dream position.

But quickly, she realized pay would be a major issue. She had managed to secure outside funding from a program, but it still wouldn't be enough.

"They told me that I was only going to be getting $2,000 for nine weeks in DC. I lived in DC last year as well and I knew for a fact that was nowhere near the amount of money I needed to be there for nine weeks. The flight from Texas to Washington, DC alone would eat up a fourth of the pay."

Hillary was resigned to the fact that she would have to dip into her savings and maybe even get another paying part-time job to complete the internship. Then the pandemic hit. For all the horrible effects the pandemic had on her and the country, the silver lining was that she completed the internship virtually from Texas. Hillary wouldn't have to worry about the money. It made her realize how absurd it was that it took something as drastic as a pandemic for her to be able to complete her government internship.

"Nothing about what happened with COVID was fortunate. It was awful. It's still awful. I was able to go into this internship, which was only open to me because of a literal once-in-a-lifetime pandemic. I think that story in of itself just showed me how high the barrier to entry is for someone like me."

To Hillary, it seemed that the federal government was purposely designed to keep individuals like her—first-generation, low-income students—out. It seems that way to me as well.

***

HISTORY OF GOVERNMENT PAY

We all accept that private sector jobs have always paid more than government jobs, but that wasn't always the case. So, when did the public sector stop competing with the private sector regarding pay?

Author of *The Meritocracy Trap: How America's Foundational Myth Feeds Inequality, Dismantles the Middle Class, and Devours the Elite*, Daniel Markovits, illustrates the history of disparate pay between the public sector and the private sector. In the early twentieth century, "Top civil servants were paid ten or even twenty times the median wage." At that time, the private sector didn't value managerial skills which the state required.[71] Naturally, the most educated and the elite went into the public sector.

Even into the mid-twentieth century, top government officials made roughly the same as their private sector counterparts. According to Markovits, "In 1969, a congressperson was paid more than he might make as a lobbyist, a federal judge received perhaps half what he might have commanded at a law firm, and the secretary of the treasury was paid a

---

71   Daniel Markovits, *The Meritocracy Trap: How America's Foundational Myth Feeds Inequality, Dismantles the Middle Class, and Devours the Elite* (New York: Penguin Press, 2019).

salary smaller than but broadly comparable to what he might have made in finance."[72]

Today, of course, the disparity is wildly greater. "A congressperson becoming a factor of ten, from $175,000 to perhaps $2 million; the chief justice of the Supreme Court earns roughly $270,000, while the very most profitable law firms pay their average partners over $5 million annually, or roughly twenty times as much ... and the secretary of the treasury earns a little more than $200,000 annually, whereas the CEOs of JPMorgan Chase, Goldman Sachs, and Morgan Stanley might average incomes of $25 million, more than a hundred times as much."[73]

This analysis only focuses on the salaries of top officials in the public sector and yet, the same idea proves true among highly driven young civil servants. In this capitalistic, career-driven, so-called meritocratic system, pay not only relates to pure compensation but also signifies worth. As young people starting out in our careers, we're looking to establish our credibility. And in this world, credibility comes from prestigious names that can pay the most.

The search for credibility drives many young people, and it's what creates the modern-day rat race. For some students, the race begins at thirteen years old. For example, in the New York City public school system, tens of thousands of middle school students take the Specialized High School Admissions Test (SHSAT) to gain entrance into one of New York

---

72 Ibid.
73 Ibid.

City's nine specialized high schools—well-known brands like Stuyvesant and Bronx Science—which are feeder schools into the Ivy League.

Once you become an Ivy League student, the race for credibility doesn't stop—you have to decide which top-tier consulting firm, investment bank, or Big Tech company will pay you the most and provide the most credibility once you graduate. And the most prestigious companies with the most well-known names will pay the most. The first-year analyst starting salary at McKinsey is between $90,000 and $120,000.[74] At bulge-bracket banks like Goldman Sachs, Wells Fargo, and UBS, the average first-year analyst starting salary is $91,000, not including bonuses.[75] And at Google, highly-sought-after software engineers can expect to make $189,000 in total compensation in their first year.[76]

The prestige and the salary of these entry-level positions are incredibly appealing to most high-achieving college students, especially to students who have spent their lives deriving their worth from external academic and professional achievements. But ultimately, the greater prestige and salary of an organization don't necessarily equate to greater societal impact. The public sector may never match private sector levels of salary, but the way we structure government

74   "Management Consultant Salary," Management Consulted, accessed February 9, 2021.
75   Reed Alexander, "From Goldman Sachs to Morgan Stanley, Here's What Bulge-Bracket Banks are Paying Their First-Year IB Analysts," *Business Insider*, August 24, 2020.
76   Kig Leswing, "Here's How Big Tech Companies Like Google and Facebook Set Salaries for Software Engineers," CNBC, June 16, 2019.

pay can certainly be improved upon to attract the next generation of public servants.

∗∗∗

THE CIVIL SERVICE

So what is the civil service and how did it become the monolith it is today?

The merit-based civil service system was first established in the United States by the passage of the Pendleton Act in 1883.[77] Before 1883, a spoils system was in place, allowing for the president to appoint any individuals to government positions. The new system under the Pendleton Act emphasized common sense and practical skills rather than the elite formal training required under the British system. The law required government employees to pass competitive civil servant tests and be chosen based on merit alone, preventing patronage and partisan behavior. The new system firmly stressed neutrality, something that current-day scholars have identified as a barrier for the public sector to hire top talent.

Since the Pendleton Act was passed in the late nineteenth century, there have been periods in time where administrations moved away from the neutrality requirement of the civil service. During the New Deal years, Franklin D. Roosevelt moved away from the strict neutrality policy of the original

---

77 George T. Milkovich, Alexander Wigdor, Renae Broderick, Anne Mavor, "Pay for Performance," *A Report Evaluating Performance Appraisal and Merit Pay* (Washington, DC: Commission on Behavioral and Social Sciences and Education, 1991).

civil servant system. He argued that government agencies should be staffed with policy experts instead of civil servants who had passed the neutrality aspects of the civil servant exams. During his tenure, the number of federal employees in the competitive civil service decreased from 80 percent to 60 percent due to policy experts taking their place.[78] In addition, the civil service exam has been abolished for several positions, as studies show the test doesn't comply with affirmative action guidelines.[79]

Then, in 1978, the Civil Service Reform Act went into effect, abolishing the United States Civil Service Commission, which was created by the Pendleton Act. The Civil Service Reform Act replaced the commission with three organizations: The Office of Management and Budget (OMB), which served as the human resources agency for the federal government; the US Merit Systems Protection Board (MSPB), which hears the appeals of federal employees regarding disciplinary matters; and the Federal Labor Relations Authority (FLRA), which oversees the rights of federal employees to form unions.

As a result of its one-hundred-plus-year history, the federal merit system has evolved into an extraordinary, complicated beast, containing both formal and informal procedures. As mentioned before, hopeful government entrants can be classified into three different categories: competitive, noncompetitive, and excepted hiring authority.

---

78 Ibid.
79 Chermerinsky, Making Sense of the Affirmative Action Debate, 22 Ohio N.U. Law Review. 1343

Competitive appointments are open to the general public and are hired through the regular application and hiring processes. Individuals who don't have an excepted hiring authority have a competitive status.[80]

Noncompetitive appointments are open to select candidates—typically federal employees with at least three years of experience—instead of the general public. Under this authority, hiring managers may hire individuals without going through the full hiring process.[81]

Excepted service is a noncompetitive subcategory that allows agencies to hire using a streamlined process rather than the regular competitive process. Agencies use this to hire hard-to-recruit positions like medical doctors and attorneys.[82]

In addition, veterans have preference in hiring. Other groups that qualify for direct hiring authority include returned Peace Corps volunteers and outstanding scholars.

The system is confusing and flawed in many ways. But to understand the flaws of the merit system, you must first understand the federal government pay scale.

***

---

80 "Glossary," Go Government, accessed August 27, 2020.
81 Ibid.
82 Ibid.

HOW DOES THE GENERAL SCHEDULE PAY SCALE WORK?

How does federal pay actually work? Unlike the more common European pay scale where pay is determined by the personal qualifications of each individual, the US system determines pay solely by the position's description and qualifications. The Classification Act of 1949 established essentially what is known as the General Schedule (GS) pay scale today.

The system consists of fifteen grades, from GS-1 to GS-15. The breakdown of the pay scale is as follows:[83]

1. **GS-1 or GS-2:** Blue collar workers with a high school degree or equivalent, between $19,543 and $27,653
2. **GS-3 or GS-4:** Typically internships or student jobs, between $23,976 and $34,988
3. **GS-5 to GS-7:** Most entry-level positions with a bachelor's degree, between $30,113 and $48,488
4. **GS-8 to GS-12:** Mid-level positions, between $41,310 and $86,021
5. **GS-13 to GS-15:** Top-level supervisory positions, between $78,681 and $142,180[84]

Beyond the GS pay scale is the Senior Executive Service (SES), a centerpiece of the Civil Service Reform Act. The SES comprises a mix of top career civil servants and political appointees. With annual salaries between $160,100 and $219,200,

---

83   "Pay and the General Schedule (GS)," Go Government, accessed August 27, 2020.
84   "How Much Does a GS-15 Employee Get Paid?" General Schedule, accessed August 27, 2020.

individuals in the SES are the highest-paid employees in the federal government.[85]

***

THE PITFALLS OF THE FEDERAL MERIT SYSTEM FOR YOUNG PEOPLE

Several substantial issues with the federal merit system affect young people and their perception of government.

First, the classification of the federal merit system hasn't been reformed since the Classification Act of 1949. This means that our federal hiring system still heavily relies on a prerequisite checklist of requirements for a position, rather than hiring based on the skills needed for the job. These often include higher education requirements and a certain number of years of experience. For many young people, especially in STEM fields, higher education and years of experience are simply not necessary to develop the skills needed for government positions.

Brandon Chin felt that way while interviewing for data scientist positions for political campaigns. He felt that political operatives didn't value his technical experience even though he could do the job.

"I got the feeling the people I talked to valued political experience more than technical experience. Most of the people

---

85   "Executive & Senior Level Employees Pay Tables," Federal Pay, accessed August 27, 2020.

I interviewed with came from less technically impressive backgrounds, but they had been in the field. They had been in politics or government longer. And I think that sort of doesn't play well with people who are in tech and are looking to like make a transition or work in politics and government."

The government merit system seems archaic and not adaptable to the needs of younger generations today.

Second, the promotional structure of the federal government is largely based on experience rather than merit. For young people who manage to break into government, this structure is highly discouraging. As one federal employee explained to me, "It's frustrating to see your fifty-year-old colleague on Facebook all day and not doing half the work you're doing, while they're at a GS-15 and you're at a GS-7."

As one government consultant described, the culture of "Time in Grade" remains in the public sector.

"There is still an unspoken perception that you must have experience at your current grade level for a certain period of time in order to get 'sufficient' experience to move up to the next grade level."[86]

In practice, if you've gotten a promotion in the past year, you likely won't be promoted for another two years. Experience still reigns king in government.

---

86   Martha Wilson, "The Ugly Truth About Promotions," *FedSmith*, January 19, 2015.

This slow-moving promotional system conflicts with Gen Z's desire for constant communication and feedback. If we excel in our jobs, we expect a positive response. Conversely, if we perform poorly, we understand the consequences. Gen Z grew up with our performance constantly being measured and tracked. Online grading portals delivered assignment grades and test results in a matter of hours; every single point we scored playing basketball in high school was recorded and posted online; every college our peers were admitted to was displayed online and used to track percentage of admissions. The idea that the federal government won't promote you for stellar work and not in a timely fashion is inherently at odds with the world Gen Z inhabits.

The argument that most proponents of government's current promotional system make is that the system prioritizes fairness above all else. The promotion system is in place so that promotions can't be based on subjective qualities and the biases of managers.

While in theory that makes sense, it ultimately works against the effectiveness of government. The current-day system places its trust in systems rather than in individuals, a concept that works against the expectations of younger generations and the private sector. While the private sector shifted toward a person-forward managing system decades ago, the public sector seems to be still stuck in a systems-forward emphasis. This not only deters employees who feel that they're simply a cog in the machine but also deters young people who want to work in government but feel their voices won't be valued. As one Department of Transportation employee puts it, "Government tries to be so fair that it inherently becomes unfair."

***

PUBLIC SERVICE LOAN FORGIVENESS

One major benefit of working for government that has proven to be highly attractive to young people is the Public Service Loan Forgiveness Program (PSLF). But while PSLF started out as an enticing incentive, today it's nothing but a fantasy.

Established under the College Cost Reduction and Access Act of 2007, PSLF enjoyed strong bipartisan support. An individual qualifies for the program after working for a qualifying government organization or nonprofit full-time for ten years after making 120 on-time monthly payments under a qualifying debt repayment program. After ten years, the rest of the individual's student debt would be forgiven.[87]

Public service loan forgiveness is a huge incentive for recent college graduates to pursue a career in the public sector. Since 2000, tuition has gone up 65 percent and 50 percent at public and private nonprofit institutions, respectively.[88] As the price of college has skyrocketed, young people have started to seriously look for alternative ways to pay for tuition. For mission-driven students, the PSLF program was the ideal

---

87   "Public Service Loan Forgiveness *Data*," Federal Student Aid, accessed August 27, 2020.

88   "College Tuition Has Increased—But What's the Actual Cost?" USA Facts, accessed August 27, 2020.

way to simultaneously pursue a career in public service while helping to pay for school.

Yet when the first cohort of PLSF participants became eligible for loan forgiveness in 2017, the program proved to be an abject failure.

Due to failed implementation of the program by the Department of Education and loopholes that make eligibility nearly impossible, 99 percent of applicants have been rejected under the current program.[89] In 2018, the Department of Education had to announce a second-chance plan for people in public service jobs who were denied loan forgiveness because they chose the wrong repayment plan.[90]

Yet the PSLF program took another hit under the Trump administration.

The Trump administration, under Education Secretary Betsy DeVos, tightened eligibility requirements for applicants. Only $10.6 million out of the $700 million appropriated by Congress has been distributed out of the PSLF Program.[91] In

89 "Gillibrand, Kaine Lead Group Of 13 Senators to Introduce New Legislation to Overhaul Flawed Public Service Loan Forgiveness Program, Ensure Millions of Americans Will Now Be Eligible for The Loan Forgiveness They Have Earned," Tim Kaine United States Senator from Virginia press release, April 11, 2019, on the Tim Kaine United States Senator from Virginia website, accessed August 27, 2020.

90 Debra Cassens Weiss, "Public Service Workers Denied Loan Forgiveness Due to Wrong Repayment Plan Given Second Chance," *ABA Journal*, May 30, 2018

91 Danielle Douglas-Gabriel, "Education Dept. Rejects Vast Majority of Applicants for Temporary Student Loan Forgiveness Program," *Washington Post*, April 2, 2019.

addition, President Trump proposed eliminating the PSLF program in both his 2018 and 2019 budget proposals.[92] Both proposals failed, yet the PSLF program remains politically controversial and at-risk for termination.

Not only is the current PSLF program untenable and highly ineffective at recruiting young people to public service, but its existence is unstable. The PSLF program not only needs to exist but must be reformed to actually be effective and appealing to young people saddled with thousands in student debt. If PSLF becomes an actual viable option, it could be a major draw for young graduates looking to enter public service.

So, what does this all mean? How do we fix issues of government pay? There are certainly steps that we can, and should, take—increasing our valuation of skills in the hiring process and promotion system and instating a public service loan forgiveness program that actually works. But the real change needed is a redefinition of worth—one that isn't so strongly tied to pay. Of course, money is immensely important. No professional would agree to work in a job for no salary whatsoever (except for government interns). But the pay of a certain job or profession should not signify its value to society. I know I sound naive and hokey, but I believe the true worth of a career should be defined not with dollars but with lives bettered. Most public servants inherently believe that. Increasingly, I believe our society is starting to as well. Changing our valuation of technical skills is a step in the

---

92   Jillian Berman, "The Trump Administration Proposes Eliminating Public Service Loan Forgiveness," *MarketWatch*, March 12, 2019.

right direction. But we need to go further. This isn't a quick fix or an easy fix, but it's a necessary one for the success of public service.

PART III

WHERE DO WE GO FROM HERE?

CHAPTER 6

THE NEW PUBLIC SECTOR TALENT PIPELINE

So, how do you recruit Gen Z? Just ask them.

Reed Shafer-Ray is the cofounder and chief operating officer for Lead for America (LFA), an organization that recruits, trains, and places outstanding recent college graduates in two-year local government fellowships. LFA is interesting for many reasons—its focus on local government, its unique recruiting practices, and its rapid growth in just two years, just to name a few. But what makes LFA truly special is that it was founded by recent college grads.

At just twenty-four, Reed's resume is an impressive one. A recent alumnus of Harvard University, Reed concentrated in social studies with a secondary concentration in mathematical sciences, graduating Magna Cum Laude with Highest Honors in 2018. While at Harvard, Reed was a leader in the political community, interning at the Massachusetts State Senate and serving as the legislative director of the Harvard College Democrats.

Reed's resume truly stands out and attracts legions of corporate recruiters. But while most of his friends and peers with similarly glowing resumes took the corporate route, Reed had a different goal in mind: local government. It was a seemingly less glamorous route, but a path that would have a much greater impact on the communities he cared about.

At Harvard, Reed first started to become disillusioned about the lack of public sector pathways available for recent college grads.

"Senior year, so many of my friends ended up taking jobs at Google and McKinsey and all these other companies. Many of them were not only brilliant but also very passionate and committed to giving back when they entered college, so many of them said they wanted to go to college to make the world a better place. Yet many of them ended up taking these jobs with no real exit plan at these giant corporations."

Reed remained convinced that if public sector pathways were better advertised, more of his friends and peers would've ended up in the public sector. The private sector was simply doing a better job of luring top talent away from public service. They offered credibility, something that government hasn't managed to figure out how to do.

To Reed, the lack of credibility in government positions made no sense. It should be reversed; "There's actually a gain in credibility and legitimacy when people take jobs in large corporations that aren't accountable to communities when, in my opinion, it should really be the opposite. The people who should be most honored or respected in society should be the people who are making the biggest difference in other people's lives—the teachers, the local government administrators, and the community organizers."

Frustrated with this systemic issue, Reed wrote a column in the student newspaper, *The Harvard Crimson*, about the systematic brain drain that happens every year at Harvard and other colleges across the country. In his opinion piece, titled *"The Tragedy of Selling Out: Trading Civic Aspirations for Six Figures,"* Reed sharply criticized the Harvard administration. "Harvard does not only neglect to provide public service opportunities for its students; its employees are also often caught making a mockery of Harvard's service-oriented mission to 'educate the citizens and citizen-leaders for our society.'"[93]

Reed's sharply worded opinion caught the attention of a senior at the University of North Carolina at Chapel Hill, Joe Nail. Joe reached out to Reed over Facebook. He shared the same frustrations—the lack of public sector pathways for college grads was demoralizing and dangerous to the future of American government. He wanted to create an organization that could fill the gap and provide a public sector pipeline for talented college grads looking to commit

---

93 Reed Shafer-Ray, "The Tragedy of Selling Out: Trading Civic Aspirations for Six Figures," *The Harvard Crimson*, November 9, 2017.

to public service. Reed was in. And a few months later, Lead for America was born.

Right from the get-go, LFA recruited differently than other public-sector-focused nonprofits or government institutions. Reed and his cofounders had all just graduated from top universities in the United States; they knew what recruiting practices were the most effective and how to best utilize them for their own purposes. So, what's the secret? According to Reed, it's not that complicated. It's about personal connection.

"I think we learned that the fundamental principle of recruiting is that you need to build that personal relationship. It sounds cliche but it's completely true and empirically validated."

LFA internalized that idea and made it their recruiting motto. As Reed explained, they used traditional recruiting methods like posting on college job boards and social media, but LFA took it much further. "By far the most effective method in terms of just numbers of applicants and where over 90 percent of our fellows have come from in the last few years is actually through us researching candidates through platforms like LinkedIn to identify the candidates who are the best possible fit."

From there, Reed and his cofounders spent hundreds of hours cultivating personal relationships with potential candidates; "We send them an email and set up a short fifteen-minute phone call, explaining the program to them and why we are reaching out to them specifically, and then just continue to follow up proactively over email or text. It's about being responsive to their questions and being flexible, working around the eligibility criteria, and making sure we are being responsive to their needs."

Much of what drove LFA to be creative with their recruiting methods was simply the fact that they had no budget. They were a bunch of twenty-two-year-olds who had just gotten limited funding from a foundation to start this ambitious nonprofit. In their first year, there was no recruiting budget. But that didn't hinder LFA whatsoever:

"A big part of it is being systematic about it and organizing recruiting on a large scale. You have to be smart about how you leverage technology and data to reach out to folks. Our first year we had no real recruitment budget. We didn't have any money to spend on ads or anything like that, so we literally found candidates on LinkedIn and bought a mail merge software for fifteen bucks. Our entire budget was no more than $2,000 and in that first year, we had eight hundred applicants. So it's not about spending a lot of money but it's about building personal relationships."

Cultivating personal relationships genuinely pays off. It's a lot more work than posting on a website or a job board and hoping for the best. In the long run, the investment of time and energy pays off in dividends. The quality of talent is greater, and the people are more passionate and committed to the organization. In short, it's worth it.

**

A BETTER PUBLIC SECTOR TALENT PIPELINE

The success of Lead for America can be replicated on a larger scale by local, state, and even federal government. LFA identified early in the process that talent needs to be constantly cultivated, which has served them well. Government is currently lacking a continuous talent pipeline.

Most agencies in the federal government simply post job openings on USAJOBS or social media and hope for the best. More proactive recruiters will show up to college fairs on campus and pitch directly to students. To ensure the future of our public sector workforce, we need an active pipeline, where young college graduates and early twenty-somethings consistently come into the federal workforce year after year. Some programs like Pathways and the Presidential Management Fellows cater to that objective, but they're not nearly effective enough or as numerous as they should be.

For example, according to a 2016 report from the Office of Personnel Management, close to half of Pathways Program Officers (PPOs) stated their agencies don't recruit beyond posting job openings to USAJOBS, largely due to budget cuts.[94] Furthermore, only 55.1 percent of agencies participate in career or college fairs.[95] This failure in outreach not only affects the quality of applicants who apply to government positions but also the perception of the public sector for college students. It's hard to understand a career in government when government fails to show up.

---

94 "The Pathways Programs: Their Use and Effectiveness Two Years After Implementation," *Special Study* (Washington, DC: US Office of Personnel Management, 2016).

95 Ibid.

Contrary to what some might believe about government, I think the public sector has all the tools necessary for a competitive recruitment process. Federal hiring managers and recruitment specialists are patriots dedicated to the common good. The issues don't lie with one specific individual or agency but, rather, are a larger, systemic problem that pervades government. I believe it's a mindset and cultural issue, where eager hiring managers feel hamstrung by the risk-adverse culture of government.

To be fair, government *should* be more risk adverse than the private sector; the problems the public sector must deal with affect the lives of millions of people in an extraordinarily consequential way. Yet there are ways to embrace new recruiting tactics that speak to Gen Z without compromising the integrity and values of the public sector. In fact, the very values of the public sector draw young people to a career in public service.

✳✳✳

A PUBLIC SECTOR TALENT PIPELINE FOR GEN Z

So what does Gen Z want out of their careers? What values do they prize above all else? Turns out, they prize the very values that comprise public service.

Gen Zers are specifically looking for three qualities on which government can capitalize: desire for stability, loan repayment, and mission-driven work.

Unlike millennials who pioneered new workplace norms and drove the flexible work revolution, Gen Z craves stability.[96] Gen Zers were children when the economic crisis in 2008 hit. Watching their parents and family members lose jobs, houses, and 401K plans made an indelible imprint on the mindsets of Gen Z. In a report done by XYZ University, two in three Gen Zers would rather have a job with financial stability than one that brings personal fulfillment.[97] A significant part of that desire for financial stability came from watching Gen Xers—their parents—lose huge amounts of wealth during the Great Recession. According to a study by the Pew Charitable Trust, members of Gen X lost 45 percent of their wealth during the Great Recession.[98] Gen Zers are determined to not be a part of that trend.

What does that mean for government?

Recruitment methods must emphasize the stability of a career in public service and the appeal of government benefits.

Of course, a career in public service can be incredibly personally fulfilling; in fact, most people I have talked to left the private sector for government because of a desire for fulfillment. Compared to the private sector, public sector positions are fairly stable apart from the occasional (or not so occasional) government shutdown. Unlike companies, the

96   Manon DeFelice, "What Gen Z Wants at Work Will Blow Your Mind," *Forbes*, October 31, 2019.

97   Josh Miller, "A 16-Year-Old Explains 10 Things You Need to Know About Generation Z," *Society for Human Resource Management*, October 30, 2018.

98   "Retirement Security Across Generations," *Report* (Washington, DC: Pew Charitable Trust, 2013).

government can't go out of business. Agencies and offices might shift and take on new forms, but there will always be government positions.

In addition, the government should also highlight its extensive benefit offerings. While public sector salaries are generally lower than private sector salaries, public sector benefits outweigh those in the private sector. According to the Congressional Budget Office, average benefits for federal employees with no more than a high school education were 93 percent higher than their counterparts in the private sector. For federal employees whose highest level of education consists of a bachelor's degree, average benefits are 52 percent higher than their private sector counterparts. Even among employees with a doctorate or professional degree, benefits average out to be roughly the same between the two sectors.[99] For Gen Zers concerned about financial stability and security, the benefits government offers are highly attractive.

For Gen Z, student debt is a major consideration when deciding on their future careers. Most Gen Zers—73 percent of them—report that they will graduate with student loan debt.[100] An overwhelming 61 percent of college students would take a job they're not passionate about due to student loan repayment pressure.[101] With college tuition higher than

---

99   Justin Falk, "Comparing the Compensation of Federal and Private sector Employees, 2011 to 2015," Report (Washington, DC: Congressional Budget Office, 2017).
100 "Survey: Student Loan Debt Is a Key Factor for Gen Z When Making Career Decisions," PR Newswire, accessed September 30, 2020.
101 Ibid.

ever, student loans are one of the biggest determinants of job selection.

As discussed in Chapter 6, a public service loan forgiveness program exists today, but it's vastly underfunded and overly complicated. The current model, established in 2007, has proven to be an abject failure, with 99 percent of applicants rejected after a decade of public service and loan payments.[102] Since 2017, there have been many political debates regarding what a better public service loan forgiveness program would look like. One such model for a new public service loan forgiveness program was proposed by President Biden while he was still running for office. The program will offer $10,000 of undergraduate or graduate debt relief for every year an individual participates in a national or community service program for up to five years. In addition, every individual working in schools, nonprofits, and government will be automatically enrolled in the loan forgiveness program. An individual could also apply for public service loan forgiveness for up to five years of prior participation in a national or community service program. Finally, this bill would ensure adjunct professors also qualify for the program, depending on how much time they've spent teaching.[103]

102 "Gillibrand, Kaine Lead Group of 13 Senators to Introduce New Legislation to Overhaul Flawed Public Service Loan Forgiveness Program" Tim Kaine United States Senator from Virginia press release, April 11, 2019.
103 "The Biden Plan for Education Beyond High School," Biden Harris, accessed September 30, 2020.

If this public service loan forgiveness program comes to fruition, it could be a major draw for young college graduates looking to enter public service.

Finally, Gen Zers are looking for mission-driven work. While most Gen Zers would take a job they're not passionate about to pay off their student debt, having work aligned with their values is also a top priority. A full 80 percent of young people say that making the world a better place is one of their top priorities.[104] In addition, Gen Zers place a high premium on diversity. Nearly half of Gen Z is non-white, and 77 percent of Gen Zers say that a company or organization's level of diversity would affect their decision to work there.[105] A company or organization's purpose and culture matter a great deal to Gen Zers.

The ability to provide meaningful, mission-driven work is perhaps government's most effective sell. Gen Zers want to do good. They want to be a part of an institution and help fight climate change or cure cancer or create policies that help the poor. Agencies should utilize top employees and their unique stories. Employees should serve as brand ambassadors, promoting their work and impact to college students and recent graduates. Hiring managers should work to research top potential candidates and cultivate relationships over a three, six, or even twelve-month period utilizing agency ambassadors. At the end of the day, it's all about the personal connection.

---

104 Hannah Sears, "Why Mission-Driven Brands are Winning in 2019," *Pixlee* (blog), April 22, 2019.
105 Ibid.

***

WHAT DOES GEN Z ULTIMATELY WANT? COMMUNITY.
On a deeper level, what every young person really yearns
for in a first job is a sense of community. A first job seems
scary—working with "real" adults, dealing with real
responsibilities at work, and lacking support and safety net.
Young people want to know that there are mentors and
colleagues looking out for them who actually care about
them as people. Private sector companies and nonprofit
organizations have tapped into that desire and have been
widely successful with it. Investment banks and management consulting firms hire in cohorts and offer extensive
personal development training and mentorship opportunities. Nonprofits like Lead for America and Teach for America also hire in cohorts, providing a sense of community
for young college grads.

Some government programs, like the Peace Corps, recruit
in cohorts as well, but not enough government agencies
take this approach. Departments typically hire when a
position is needed, not on a recurring, consistent timeline
and not multiple people at once. Agencies should adjust
their structure to allow young people to enter government
service on a cohort basis. In addition, government agencies should work to formalize mentorship programs and
professional development. For example, a common interest
among young graduates is applying or pursuing graduate
school after a few years in the workforce. Agency leaders
could work to match graduates of particular schools with
prospective students to advise younger workers on their

applications or shed a light on what the experience is like. Through acts of connection like this, both younger and more experienced employees share a sense of community and feel a part of the larger agency.

Finally, the federal government must work to recruit underrepresented minorities and nontraditional candidates. Diversity is critical for any organization, but even more vital for the government. Our public institutions should reflect the makeup of our country. Federal agencies should expand their efforts, recruiting from historically black institutions as well as schools that serve refugees, minority populations, and nontraditional students. In addition, a growing number of individuals in the United States forego traditional education for alternative training programs. The government already spends huge amounts of money—nearly $19 billion—on training programs to help people develop practical skills for careers.[106] Agencies should partner with those programs to hire quality talent.

Above all else, the most successful recruitment model is Reed's motto at Lead for America: build personal relationships. The federal government can seem incredibly impersonal and far removed from the day-to-day lives of individuals, but it doesn't have to be like that. Personal connection drives us all. It's the one true quality that every person is looking for. Government can and should tap into it.

---

106 Adam Millsap, "Upskilling Workers for the Post-Pandemic Economy," *Forbes*, September 4, 2020.

CHAPTER 7

THE CIVIC TECH MOVEMENT

———

Todd Park fell into public service accidentally.

As the cofounder of a successful health care technology company, Athenahealth, Park seems to be the stereotypical tech start-up entrepreneur—exceedingly bright, intensely dedicated, and fiercely loyal to the West Coast. But his biography suggests another breed of tech guru altogether—one that refuses to be duty-bound to Silicon Valley: a civic tech entrepreneur.

Park was born in 1973 in Ohio, the son of a chemical engineer who emigrated from South Korea. Park credits his father with inspiring him to tackle large, systemic problems and instilling in him a strong work ethic. As he told *The Atlantic*, "A kid never listens to what his parents tell him to do. The parents act as an example of what their kids themselves do. He worked non-stop. He worked day and night. And he worked weekends … He was an example to me and my brother of a person who was genuinely consumed by his work."[107]

Park excelled academically and went on to study economics at Harvard. While at Harvard, he took a course called Public Sector Economics with a professor named David Cutler. In this class, Park first realized the magnitude of issues that plague the health care industry. The problem that frustrated Park the most was that so many of these complex issues could be solved with innovative approaches. The problem wasn't a lack of innovators in the health care sector; in fact, many health-care-focused entrepreneurs were determined to fix health care in the United States. The issue was with the system itself.

Today in the health care industry, insurance companies pay for health care on a per-service basis. Each treatment has a specific cost, providing an incentive for doctors to perform a greater number of procedures.

In cofounding Athenahealth, Park attempted to invert the model. His first forays with Athenahealth included trying to reduce costly complications with pregnant mothers by assigning each mother a doctor, midwife, nutritionist, and case manager.

While insurance companies would have to pay slightly more upfront, ultimately, the comprehensive care reduced complications, which reduced costs by as much as 20 percent.[108]

---

107 Simon Owens, "Can Todd Park Revolutionize the Health Care Industry?" The Atlantic, June 2, 2011.
108 Ibid.

However, when Park approached major insurance companies proposing his new model of payment, they couldn't accommodate his innovative idea. The insurance companies were stuck in their rigid model of paying on a per-service basis. Even though they agreed that Park's new system was more effective for all parties, the system simply didn't allow for a new payment method. Park's idea couldn't be effective if it couldn't scale.

Eventually, Athenahealth pivoted toward creating medical management software and online services. A decade after Park cofounded the company at twenty-four, Athenahealth's market capitalization exceeded $1 billion.[109] In 2018, Athenahealth sold to two private equity firms for $5.47 billion in cash.[110] Park left the firm in 2008, intending on retiring at the ripe old age of thirty-six. His wife, Amy, who he had met at Harvard, just had a child and Park intended to spend the rest of his life as a passive investor and father. Life seemed set.

Then in 2009, the federal government came calling. In June, Bill Corr, the deputy secretary of Health and Human Services (HHS) emailed, asking Park to become chief technology officer (CTO) of HHS. Park was hesitant. He had just retired after working ten years nonstop on Athenahealth and he had a newborn at home. But Corr convinced Park that he wouldn't just be the head of IT at HHS; Park would serve as HHS's first "entrepreneur in residence," harnessing tech and data to make government more transparent. This was the beginning of the civic tech movement.

---

109 Ibid.
110 Allison Prang, "Athenahealth to Sell Itself for $5.47 Billion," *Wall Street Journal*, November 12, 2018.

President Obama made revolutionizing government through technology a major administration priority from day one of his tenure. On his first day in office, President Obama issued a memorandum on transparency and open government where he declared, "Openness will strengthen our democracy and promote efficiency and effectiveness in government."[111]

Park's job was to implement that objective for HHS. Despite his recent retirement status, Park took the position. As the CTO of the federal agency charged with protecting the health of all Americans, Park found himself in the unique position to affect change in the health care system he had butted heads with at Harvard and as a young entrepreneur. The opportunity was too compelling to pass up.

Park immediately got to work at HHS. Using both his Silicon Valley and newfound government connections, in March of 2009, Park met with forty-five health care and tech leaders and told them HHS would begin to release huge amounts of data from HHS and its subagencies. He asked them to spend ninety days analyzing the data and building applications and tools that could be used to improve health care across the country. After three months, the ones that succeeded would be asked to present their ideas at the inaugural Community Health Data Initiative Forum.

Harnessing the data of the federal government and skill sets of the private sector worked. After three months, the people he met with came back and presented twenty different tools utilizing the data from HHS. Projects included Microsoft's

111 Luke Fretwell, "A Brief History of Open Data," *FCW*, June 9, 2014.

Hospital Compare, which links patient satisfaction of hospitals to their search engine, Bing, for people to determine the best quality hospitals, and an app called iTriage, which allows users to type in a medical treatment and find the closest community health center (which provides health care for uninsured individuals) that performs the procedure. Altogether, the tools created using the data from HHS resulted in tens of thousands of users and saved the government millions of dollars. Park challenged the operational model of government and proceeded to create change within ninety days. It was revolutionary.

Not only did Park revolutionize the processes of the federal government, but he changed the working culture of HHS. Using his Silicon Valley pedigree, Park ran his department like a start-up. Deadlines were shortened, projects were fast-paced, and new ideas were constantly being generated. The practices of the tech world and the practices of twenty and thirty-year-olds were coming to the federal government.

From 2012 to 2014, President Obama appointed Park as the US Chief Technology Officer, where he oversaw the application of new technologies throughout the entire federal government. During his tenure, Park spearheaded numerous initiatives including the creation of the Presidential Innovation Fellows, the beginnings of the US Digital Service, and, perhaps most notably, oversaw the fixing and relaunch of the Healthcare.gov website in 2013.[112]

---

112 Colby Hochmuth, "US CTO Stepping Down," *FCW*, August 22, 2014.

The tangible benefits Park brought to Washington, DC are quite clear and extremely impressive. But Park brought more than tech ingenuity and cost-saving measures to the federal government; he inspired an entire movement of esteemed civically minded technologists—a movement that's rapidly changing not only the processes of the public sector but the very culture of government itself: the civic tech movement.

***

WHAT IS THE CIVIC TECH MOVEMENT?

The exact definition of civic tech is hard to pin down simply because the field encompasses so many factors. Broadly speaking, civic tech is defined as technologies that are built and deployed to enhance relationships between people and government as well as technology tools built to improve government effectiveness.[113] Sometimes the term GovTech is used to separately define technology used by government solely to improve internal efficiency and effectiveness, but we'll be using civic tech to encompass both definitions.

We'll be looking at how the civic tech movement has influenced government practices, focusing on the sudden influx of technology-focused programs cropping up in the federal government system. These programs—like the Presidential Innovation Fellows, US Digital Service, and 18F—are relatively small, especially given the sheer size of the federal government. But their impact has far outstripped their diminished numbers. In less than a decade, this small cohort

---

113 Quora, "What Is Civic Technology?" *Forbes*, September 19, 2017.

of technologists have been responsible for hundreds of millions of cost-saving measures, generated hundreds of creative ideas, and connected the public and private sector in ways never seen before.

But outside the external successes of the civic tech community, technology leaders have also transformed the internal practices of the federal government. In bringing private sector expertise to the public sector, technologists have learned how to blend best practices in the tech community and accountability metrics in the public sector. In addition, civic tech programs have implemented their own highly successful recruitment and hiring procedures that have started to influence the hiring practices of other agencies as well.

Why is the civic tech movement so important? Why should we care about a few programs that account for an almost negligible percentage of the federal workforce?

Because civic tech practices represent the best of what government could be. Now, not every agency can or should be run like a start-up in Silicon Valley. For all the complaints about government being slow and bureaucratic, people forget that government is slow and bureaucratic for a reason. Democracy requires that every voice be heard in equal measure. And system-wide changes that affect at least 330 million people require careful considerations and inputs. But the federal government can improve in several areas: recruitment can be more targeted, hiring can be more streamlined, and the work can be more suited for the Digital Age.

Ultimately, the civic tech movement represents the future. The average age of a Google employee is twenty-nine years old.[114] That means the best practices of Silicon Valley mirror the most desired practices of many young people. Furthermore, the public sector desperately needs to recruit more young, tech-savvy individuals. For the federal government, having top tech talent isn't a matter of competing in a market—it's a matter of national security, a matter of democratic protection, and a matter of life and death. It's not enough to rely on the successes of the current civic tech movement. For government to survive in the twenty-first century, the civic tech movement needs to expand rapidly and significantly to include increasing numbers of young people. Our future literally depends on it.

***

HISTORY OF THE CIVIC TECH MOVEMENT

It's difficult to pinpoint a specific start date for the civic tech movement, as most civic tech insiders name different dates. But everyone can point out the person who started it all: President Obama.

In tech circles, Obama's ascendancy to the presidency in 2009 was a moment of pure excitement and hope. Obama was seen to be a tech-anointed god, more than any other politician had ever been. Cool, calm, and collected, he had the ease of a laid-back California software engineer but the sharp

---

114 Max Nisen, "A 64-year-old Engineer is Suing Google for Age Discrimination," *Quartz*, April 24, 2015.

intellect of a Big Tech business leader. But more importantly, he knew his stuff. Obama was almost as adept at talking about artificial intelligence and the importance of data as he was talking about politics.

The Obama Foundation accurately deemed President Obama as "Our First Tech President."[115] I couldn't agree more. But in Obama's first term, that title didn't seem like a foregone conclusion. While Obama came into office espousing the importance of open data and government transparency, he fell short of the high expectations of tech policy experts. While Obama made some incremental changes to tech policies, creating new roles—including chief technology officer, chief information officer, and chief data officer—technologists wanted big, sweeping reforms. To be fair, Obama had other issues to contend with, including a major economic recession, national security threats, and a highly polarized Congress. Tech would have to take a (temporary) backseat.

Then in 2012, at the start of Obama's second term, Todd Park became Obama's second CTO. Like he did at HHS, Park revolutionized the White House's outlook on the usefulness of tech.

One of Park's first major accomplishments was launching the Presidential Innovation Fellows (PIF) program, a small cohort of technologists who serve "tours of duty" within various agencies in the federal government. This group of tech

---

115 Steven Levy, "The Final Days of Obama's Tech Surge," *Wired*, January 10, 2017.

leaders were highly accomplished individuals at the top of their respective fields.

The inclusion of Presidential Innovation Fellows (or PIFs as they're known) in the federal government served two primary objectives. One, by making the program highly selective and top caliber, PIF became well-known and reputable in the tech community, allowing it to continuously attract top talent. Second, in addition to becoming creditable within the private sector, PIF garnered respect and trust among career public servants. Once government employees realized that PIFs delivered high-impact solutions within a shortened time frame, a mutual appreciation began to form. Furthermore, over half of the 150 fellows that have served since the program's inception in 2012 have remained in government.[116] Once many private sector stalwarts got a taste of a mission-driven career, it was too difficult to go back.

The "Tech Surge" snowballed from there.[117] Soon after the inaugural year of PIF, a group of fellows decided to expand their influence and founded 18F, a team of technologists that work within the General Services Administration (GSA). GSA is the government agency charged with constructing and maintaining government buildings—18F's 120 employees collaborate with other agencies to fix technical problems, build products, and find technical solutions to improving government efficiency. The civic tech movement was expanding quickly.

---

116 "Our First Tech President," Our Story, Obama Foundation, accessed September 25, 2020.

117 "Who We Are," About, Presidential Innovation Fellows, accessed September 25, 2020.

And yet, the Tech Surge may have never happened without the biggest tech disaster of the Obama presidency. When the Affordable Care Act (ACA) passed in 2010, it became the greatest legislative victory of Obama's tenure. Millions of people in the United States gained access to health insurance and individuals with pre-existing conditions no longer had to fear being denied health insurance. However, after the passage of the ACA, a much larger problem began to emerge: how would the federal government handle the logistics of overhauling health care?

In short, not well.

Obama decided to tackle the logistics of the ACA from a traditional federal government perspective, appointing Nancy-Ann DeParle, director of the White House Office of Health Reform, to lead the bill's implementation. Top White House advisors warned him against a purely governmental approach. According to *The Washington Post*, Obama health care advisor Zeke Emanuel "lobbied for the president to appoint an outside health reform 'czar' with expertise in business, insurance, and technology."[118] Obama's closest economic advisor, Larry Summers, shared Emmanuel's concern as well. But Obama was insistent: the implementation of the ACA would be done in-house.

The result was a disaster. When HealthCare.gov was released on October 1, 2013, it crashed within two hours of its launch.[119]

---

118 Steven Levy, "The Final Days of Obama's Tech Surge," *Wired*, January 10, 2017.

119 Amy Goldstein and Juliet Eilperin, "HealthCare.gov: How Political Fear Was Pitted against Technical Needs," *Washington Post*, November 2, 2013.

The website was designed as a health care marketplace, allowing users to compare insurance plans and sign up for the best fit. But almost no one could even get past the login system; the capacity wasn't there. On the website's first day, only six people were able to sign up for insurance.[120] It was an unmitigated train wreck.

In a panic, the administration tapped Park to fix the situation. However, when Park began to assess the damage with some other PIFs, he realized that advisors like Emanuel and Summers had been correct: this problem couldn't be solved solely through the resources of the federal government alone. Using his connections from Silicon Valley and the Obama campaign, Park managed to cultivate a small group of coders and developers to fix the issue in a matter of weeks.[121] Park now had the attention of White House officials; government needed tech talent desperately.

According to Steven Levy in an article in *Wired*, "HealthCare. gov did not become Obama's Katrina, but, rather, his pivot into a full and lusty embrace of tech culture."[122] Park seized upon the momentum and began to establish the US Digital Service (USDS), a group of established technology experts who work in numerous federal agencies to increase effectiveness and fix some of the federal government's largest issues.[123] In just seven years, USDS has proven to be a resounding

---

120 Frank Thorp, "Only 6 Able to Sign Up on Healthcare.gov's First Day, Documents Show," NBC News, October 31, 2013.
121 Amy Goldstein, "HHS Failed to Heed Many Warnings That HealthCare. gov Was in Trouble," *Washington Post*, February 23, 2016.
122 Steven Levy, "The Final Days of Obama's Tech Surge," *Wired*, January 10, 2017.
123 Ibid.

success. Some of its most impactful projects have included rebuilding the VA.gov website to make it more simplified and consolidated, improving VA software reliability (resulting in nearly $100 million in cost-savings), and making it easier for military families to relocate.[124] It looks like civic tech is here to stay.

***

LESSONS FROM CIVIC TECH

Out of the myriad initiatives civic tech programs have undertaken these past years, one in particular stands out—USDS's focus on improving federal recruitment government-wide. The work USDS is doing looks promising. Their proposed reforms are not only highly effective but also compatible with what young people are looking for in a hiring process. With a lot of work and a bit of luck, recruiting reforms might be coming soon.

In 2019, the Office of Personnel Management and USDS teamed up to examine federal hiring practices and determine how to best improve them. They launched hiring pilot programs in two agencies, the Department of the Health & Human Services and the National Park Service, to better assess applicants' qualifications.[125] The program had two primary objectives: to evaluate qualified candidates more effectively and to shorten the timeline, with quality assessment being of the utmost priority. As Stephanie Grosser, a

---

124 "How We Work," US Digital Service, accessed September 26, 2020.
125 Nick Sinai, "Congress Should Grow the Digital Services Budget, Which More Than Pays for Itself," *The Hill*, May 17, 2019.

"bureaucracy hacker" with USDS, said at an event with the National Academy of Public Administration, "You have to get the quality right and then speed that process up once you have a process that works."[126]

For the pilot programs, OPM and USDS established a new set of guidelines for agency hiring managers and human resource specialists. The first step, instrumental for ensuring quality candidate screening, was for agencies to select subject-matter experts (SMEs) to help screen for candidates for a specific position.

Under the new hiring system, no candidate is considered qualified until they pass two interviews with SMEs designed to test specific competencies. While this new process may look intensive and unappealing to potential applicants, it correlates to the typical job interviews young people expect in the private sector. Because the newly designed process invokes a sense of familiarity, young people would be more comfortable going through the hiring process and, therefore, more likely to apply. Furthermore, this new system emphasizes skill set over experience, which young people are more accustomed to, especially within tech.

Once qualification determinations are made, agencies can then prioritize veterans in the selection process. After that decision is made, agencies rate the candidates and human resources specialists can make a list of qualified candidates for the hiring manager to choose from. Overall, the process

---

126 Nicole Ogrysko, "Agencies Find Higher Quality Candidates Under New Digital Service, OPM Hiring Pilot," Federal News Network, October 25, 2019.

is greatly streamlined and simplified, easing the complications of federal hiring that have notoriously plagued the government. Even more salient, the pilot hiring process shifts priorities compared to the traditional federal hiring process. Instead of hiring primarily based on experience, the new hiring process hires primarily based on skill. This will not only allow for the federal government to compete with the private sector for top talent but would also attract significantly more young people to public service.

On a numbers basis, the pilot programs were a resounding success. According to an article in the Federal News Network, "In the past, it took hiring managers up to forty-seven days to make these selections. But under the new process, pilot agencies took between eleven and sixteen days to choose from a list of qualified candidates."[127]

The number of qualified candidates was significantly reduced, with just 11 percent of candidates who applied for an IT position at the National Park Service deemed qualified out of more than 220 applicants.[128] However, while the number of qualified candidates was lower due to the program's more intensive qualification process, there wasn't a marked impact on any particular demographic. According to Grosser, "Again, we applied veteran's preference only at the end. Four veterans made it through the process. In both processes, federal employees made it through, private sector applicants made it through, people under thirty made it through, women made

---

127 Ibid.
128 Ibid.

it through [and] different racial groups made it through."[129] The process is tough, without a doubt, but fair.

While the pilot represents the very beginning stages of recruitment reform, change is slowly starting to take form. USDS presented the new hiring strategy at twenty agencies in 2019. At least five agencies are piloting versions of the new hiring processes on their own.[130] Change happens incrementally, but any movement brings a glimmer of hope to public sector hopefuls. Especially young people.

***

YOUNG PEOPLE IN CIVIC TECH

What about young people? How do we get them into civic tech?

Young people already dominate the tech sector. The average age of tech employees at the largest firms in the country hovers around age thirty. And while PIFs, 18F employees, and USDS employees are typically fairly young, early twenty-year-olds don't populate their ranks like twenty-somethings do in Silicon Valley companies.

Why?

Again, it's not an issue of interest. In recent years, civic tech organizations focusing specifically on young people have

---

129 Ibid.

130 Nicole Ogrysko, "2020 is the Year for Scaling Up Trump Administration Workforce Pilots," Federal News Network, January 9, 2020.

started to crop up—groups like Coding It Forward, which was founded in 2017 by a group of technology students who were frustrated with the lack of mission-driven technical internships. They created the Civic Digital Fellowship, a government internship for technical students.[131] Nonprofits like TechCongress, which is a start-up nonprofit, incubated at the Open Technology Institute at the think tank New America. TechCongress operates the Congressional Innovation Scholars program, which places recent technical degree grads on Capitol Hill for ten months.[132]

But ultimately, nonprofits can't fill the gap of young tech talent in the federal government. That's why a government-supported civic tech program like USDS is needed, specifically designed for twenty-somethings. The needs of young people looking for their first jobs are unique. The federal government knows this, which is why programs like the Pathways Program and the Workforce Recruitment Program exist.

Young people need opportunities for formal and informal mentorship, growth, and extensive training. But the payoffs for creating a civic tech program for young people far outweigh the initial investment required. If a USDS-like program existed for recent college grads and young people with technical skills, the federal government would be able to cultivate a strong talent pipeline, powering the future federal workforce for decades. For the federal government to compete in a complex digital world, it needs young tech talent. This is the way to get it.

---

131 "Our Story," Coding it Forward, accessed September 27, 2020.
132 "About Us," TechCongress, accessed September 27, 2020.

Civic tech leaders today recognize the issue and are already working on it. Clare Martorana, chief information officer at the Office of Personnel and Management, told me that her long-term goal is to bring the next ten thousand young technologists into government, including both college grads and talented technical individuals who have chosen not to pursue a four-year degree. She and other civic-tech enthusiasts envision a "USDS meets Teach for America" program that recruits widely and as diversely as possible, but also as intensely and vigorously as possible to bring the best and brightest into public service.

Presidential Innovation Fellow, Clarice Chan, is also working to recruit a generation of technologists into government service. On civic leave from Microsoft to complete her Presidential Innovation Fellowship, Clarice wants more technology firms to offer civic leave. In fact, Microsoft is thought to have the most advanced civic leave policy. Employees with two years of work experience at the company and a good performance history are eligible to take leave for up to eighteen months, pending approval.[133]

But considering the nascent age of the tech industry, most companies have yet to develop extensive civic leave policies. In 2018, the White House hosted a summit for more than 150 tech leaders from companies like Amazon, Apple, and Adobe, among others, to promote civic leave. A norm and culture of civic leave in the tech industry would, without a doubt, improve government effectiveness, especially given

133 Tajha Chappellet-Lanier, "The White House Wants to Make Civic Leave for Technologists Normal and Accessible. Will it Take Off?" *FedScoop*, October 24, 2018.

the lack of tech talent in the federal workforce currently. In addition, a civic leave norm would be highly appealing to young people looking to do good.

It's also important to note that civic tech doesn't just apply to software engineers and product managers. In a report titled, *Corporate Civic Responsibility: A New Paradigm for Companies to Advance Public Interest Technology,* Clarice emphasizes that corporate civic responsibility also encompasses marketing, sales, and HR professionals.[134] Civic leave can and should be expanded to include tech professionals of all backgrounds.

Young people don't expect to stay at one organization for their entire career and are already extremely mission-driven, but often, they feel that their interest in private sector tech work and government service are mutually exclusive. Civic leave allows for young people to have both experiences while fulfilling their desire to affect societal change.

The ultimate goal of several prominent stakeholders is to make public interest technology as ubiquitous as public interest law. The development of public interest law didn't happen out of the blue but, rather, as a result of a concerted effort by a team of nonprofits, most namely the Ford Foundation. Before the Ford Foundation began investing in public interest law, that field primarily consisted of legal aid and legal defense clinics.

---

134 "Corporate Civic Responsibility: A New Paradigm for Companies to Advance Public Interest Technology," Report (Washington, DC: Ford Foundation and Tech Talent Project, 2020).

Beginning in the 1960s, Ford began to invest in foundational publications as well as helped to establish the Mexican American Legal Defense and Education Fund (MALDEF) and the Native American Rights Fund (NARF).[135] Ford's investment served as a catalyst for legal aid clinic programs founded by Harvard law professor Jeanne Charn and Berkeley law professor Jeffrey Selbin.[136] By the late 1980s, the Ford Foundation helped support the creation of the American Bar Association's (ABA) Law Firm Pro Bono Project; the ABA credits the program as helping to establish pro bono norms in law firms.

Now, the Ford Foundation and other organizations like the Mozilla Foundation, Media Democracy Fund, and New America, aim to do the same with public interest technology. Through private and public sector partnerships, the goal is to harness technology and the talent of technologists to solve some of the world's most complicated problems. Already, public interest tech leaders have worked on pressing issues like algorithm bias, online surveillance, and free expression.[137] And the civic tech movement is just getting started. With continued momentum and significant input from young people, the impact of technology on society will be enormous.

135 "Building a New Field of Public Interest Technology: Lessons Learned from Public Interest Law," Research Report (Washington, DC: Ford Foundation, 2018).

136 Ibid.

137 "Individuals," Public Interest Tech, Ford Foundation, accessed September 27, 2020.

CHAPTER 8

HOW THE COVID-19 PANDEMIC WILL CHANGE PUBLIC SERVICE

It's difficult for any book written in 2020 not to mention the COVID-19 pandemic. Much has been said and will be said about this period of time. For the first time in my life, I'm cognizant of the fact that I'm living through a transformative historical moment—a moment that will be written about in the history textbooks of the future. One day, many months or years from now, we as a society will collectively look back at this harrowing period and note the preconceived notions and facets of our country that changed due to the pandemic— some bad, some good, some really bad, and some really good. I don't know what we as a country or as a world will look like after we reemerge from this nightmare, but I can guarantee we'll all be different. As the ancient philosopher Heraclitus once famously said, "Into the same rivers we step and do not step, we are and are not."[138] In other words, the only constant in life is change.

The negative effects of this pandemic will be written about extensively. But a positive change I predict is a renaissance in public service—a rediscovered steadfast belief in service to family, community, and country. The pandemic has renewed my own belief in service and my faith in the best of humanity.

I started the year 2020 in Washington, DC, a new city with new friends. On a whim during freshman year, I applied for a study abroad program called Penn in Washington, where a cohort of University of Pennsylvania students spent a semester in Washington, DC interning full-time and taking classes at night. It made sense—the program fit my background and interests perfectly. I was a philosophy, politics, and economics (PPE) major with an undying love for constitutional law and foreign policy. Washington, DC was the epicenter of everything I was interested in.

I thought a career in government seemed perfect, but I didn't have a clue what that meant in real life. No one I knew had ever worked in the public sector. Furthermore, all the private sector stalwarts in my life (and there were many) trashed government. They told me the public sector was inefficient, ineffective, and paid terribly. I figured before I committed my life to working in government, I should at least see if they were right.

---

138 Daniel W. Graham, "Heraclitus," *Stanford Encyclopedia of Philosophy*, September 3, 2019.

So, I was dropped in Washington, DC in early January 2020 with seventeen other Penn students, all of us completely clueless. I fell in love with the city immediately. Washington, DC continuously vibrates with intellectual energy. You can feel it whether you're riding the Metro or walking the neighborhoods or standing in front of the Washington Monument. But as amazing as the city is, I truly fell in love with the people.

As college students, we got unique and rare access to some of the most accomplished and talented public servants in the country. As a nineteen-year-old, I had the opportunity to meet them in all facets of my day-to-day life. They were my coworkers, my bosses, my professors, guest lecturers, think tank panelists, or random coffee chat partners. I asked every one of them—and there must have been hundreds—if they enjoyed working in the public sector. And every one of them did. I was expecting to hear at least some of them complain about how little they got paid or how bureaucratic the government was. And sure, people complained about all those factors, but people loved their work. They loved serving a mission larger than themselves, loved pursuing an ideal they were incredibly passionate about. I was stunned. I was inspired.

And then suddenly, in the middle of March, my friends and I were yanked out of Washington, DC and forced to return home. A pandemic hit slowly and then all at once. On a Wednesday, we received an email from the University of Pennsylvania that the rest of the semester would be conducted online. On Friday, I was back home.

Being back home in the middle of a lockdown was a culture shock. In Washington, DC, I felt near people making an impact on the world. At home, I felt cut off from that feeling and embroiled in a sense of helplessness. My home, New York, felt like it was teetering on the precipice of a cliff. The month of April seemed to be the end of New York City. Hospitals were overrun and people were dying in increments of thousands a day. Our superheroes—doctors, nurses, and essential workers—were suffering from emotional and physical anguish. Kids stopped learning. Parents struggled to feed their kids. I was overwhelmed by the magnitude of the problem.

Samantha Power, the former ambassador to the UN under President Obama, has a saying: "Shrink the Change."[139] Whenever you feel too small to solve a big problem, take one small step. As Power describes, "It takes many small steps over time to make a dent in the larger issue."[140] I took that saying to heart. I couldn't cure coronavirus, eliminate hunger, or prevent job loss. I couldn't close the education gap that would inevitably develop because of this pandemic. But I could do my part. So, in April, I started tutoring a fifth grader over Zoom. It was just an hour a week, reading the Harry Potter series and helping her improve her reading skills, but it meant the world to me. I felt like I was being useful, impactful. Despite the utter darkness enveloping me, I clung to my sliver of light.

---

139 "Samantha Power: Change what Seems Possible," Lehigh News, October 24, 2018.
140 Ibid.

All around me, people were clinging to their slivers of light as well. People were donating to food pantries, sewing face masks, and virtually reading stories to kids. People were rediscovering what service meant—fidelity to neighbors, to communities, to country. I believe that sense of fidelity will continue long past the tragedies of COVID-19.

I reconnected with what it means to serve. Service isn't a grand, abstract concept only associated with presidents and ambassadors and career politicians. It's about helping a struggling student with their homework. It's about delivering groceries to elderly neighbors. It's about cooking a meal for a high-risk neighbor. It's about small measures of kindness and fidelity that add up to a collective impact. Other people reconnected with that ideal as well. That's why I think we'll see a renaissance in public service; people remember what it is like to be a part of a team larger than themselves, fighting against a common enemy.

***

TRUST AND PUBLIC SERVICE

I've cited many tangible factors causing the shortage of young people in government: high barriers to entry, ineffective recruiting tactics, long onboarding times, and low pay. But a crucial intangible factor that has a monumental impact on the number of young people in public service is the *perception* of government. And the greatest indicator we have regarding the perception of government is levels of trust. Trust in government—particularly the federal government—is inextricably linked to levels of public service. Young people want to work for a purpose, and government is theoretically supposed to embody that. But trust in government has fallen dramatically in the last few decades, which has affected the perception of government and, subsequently, the amount of young people going into government.

Public trust in the federal government has been extremely low these past few years, but it wasn't always this dismal .[141] When Eisenhower was president, about three-quarters of Americans said they trusted the federal government to do the right thing.[142] Since 2008, that number hasn't risen above 25 percent.[143]

Despite all the evidence to the contrary, I believe government trust will increase post-COVID-19. Not all at once, but gradually, government will start to give us a reason to trust it again. While issues of trust didn't originate with the Trump Administration, it has certainly declined because of it. Throughout his presidency, Trump consistently attacked key governmental institutions, including those that are vital when facing a national health crisis. Political experts hope that Americans will realize Trump's actions have had severe consequences. As Michiko Kakutani, author of the 2018 bestseller, *The Death of Truth*, predicted, "The coronavirus pandemic, one hopes, will jolt Americans into a realization that the institutions and values Donald Trump has spent his presidency assailing

141 "Americans' Views of Government: Low Trust, but Some Positive Performance Ratings," Pew Research Center, September 14, 2020.

142 Sabrina Tavernise, "Will the Coronavirus Kill What's Left of Americans' Faith in Washington?" *The New York Times*, May 23, 2020.

143 Ibid.

are essential to the functioning of a democracy—and to its ability to grapple effectively with a national crisis."[144]

When the director of the CDC, Robert Redfield, testified before a Senate committee in September 2020 that a vaccine would not be widely available until the middle of 2021, the president quickly attacked the scientific studies of the CDC; "I think he made a mistake when he said that. It's just incorrect information."[145]

In addition, Trump slammed Dr. Anthony Fauci, the director of the National Institute of Allergy and Infectious Diseases, who testified that the US has seen more cases than European countries because it only shut down a fraction of the economy in response to the pandemic. After Dr. Fauci testified, Trump tweeted, "Wrong! We have more cases because we have tested far more than any other country, 60 million. If we tested less, there would be less cases."[146] Trump's comments are symptoms of a larger trend of political figures sowing distrust in government institutions. While this is concerning in normal times, it's downright dangerous during times of national crisis.

Yet the pandemic has already made people realize the importance of science and truth, especially from our government institutions. In a Quinnipiac University poll released in July 2020, 65 percent of respondents said they trusted the

144 Michiko Kakutani, "Coronavirus Will Change the World Permanently. Here's How," *POLITICO Magazine*, April 15, 2020.

145 Evan Semones, "'Wrong!': Trump Slams Fauci over Testimony on Covid-19 Surge," *POLITCO Magazine*, August 1, 2020.

146 Ibid.

information Fauci provided about the virus, while just 30 percent of respondents said they trusted information from Trump. Trust in governments, both here in the US and around the world, actually surged during the pandemic.[147] According to the Edelman Trust Barometer report, people are putting their trust in governments around the world to lead them through the coronavirus pandemic. In the United States, 46 percent of people trusted the federal government "to do what is right."[148]

This will be a pivotal point for levels of trust in this country, and as trust in government rises, so will levels of young people working in government. It will take time; it will take a concerted effort by politicians, government officials, and the media to restore trust in this country. But I believe it will happen, and that will have a profound effect on the level of young people working in government.

***

THE ERA OF SMALL GOVERNMENT IS OVER

Another effect of the pandemic is the heightened visibility of government. The battle against coronavirus has risen the profiles of certain public figures rarely seen before. Dr. Fauci became a household name. In a six-day period in March 2020—at the height of the pandemic in New York—more than 4.7 million people tuned in to watch New York Governor Andrew Cuomo's daily briefings, not counting cable

---

147 Lucy Handley, "Trust in Governments Surges during Pandemic but People Are Disappointed with CEO Performance," CNBC, May 5, 2020.
148 Ibid.

watchers.[149] Government's role in the day-to-day lives of Americans has risen dramatically.

Because of all of this, political experts predict the COVID-19 pandemic will put an end to the era of small government as initiated by the Reagan era. Lilliana Mason, associate professor of government and politics at the University of Maryland, College Park, stated, "The widely accepted idea that government is inherently bad won't persist after coronavirus. This event is global evidence that a functioning government is crucial for a healthy society."[150]

The role of government has already expanded massively and suddenly in response to the pandemic. As of October 5, 2020, the US government has spent four trillion dollars responding to the coronavirus, making it the costliest economic relief effort in recent history.[151] Despite the costly stimulus, four trillion dollars was still not enough to revive the US economy or to help the least fortunate among us. For example, the $670 billion Paycheck Protection Program (PPP), which provided loans to businesses to pay employees, did not compel business owners to protect paychecks, and many owners failed to do so.[152] According to a report by economists at MIT, PPP

---

149 Mark Weiner, "Digital Views for Cuomo's Daily Coronavirus Briefings Set Records," Syracuse.com, March 31, 2020.

150 Lilliana Mason, "Coronavirus Will Change the World Permanently. Here's How," POLITICO Magazine, April 15, 2020.

151 Peter Whoriskey and Douglas MacMillan, "'Doomed to Fail': Why a $4 Trillion Bailout Couldn't Revive the American Economy," The Washington Post, October 5, 2020.

152 Ibid.

only saved about 2.31 million jobs at $224,000 each.[153] To put that in perspective, 2.4 million people filed for benefits the week just before the report was released.[154]

The COVID-19 pandemic has exposed the weaknesses of American society, due to years of hollowing out federal agencies and steadily increasing income inequality. Now more than ever, Americans are turning to government for their economic survival.

The government has also recorded higher levels of trust than businesses during the pandemic. In January 2020, the Edelman Trust Barometer registered business as the most trusted institution, whereas government and the media were tied for the least trusted institution. However, in May 2020, amid the COVID-19 outbreak, governments were registered as the most trustworthy institution compared to businesses, nonprofits, and the media.[155]

People surveyed in the study were disappointed with the actions of CEOs during the pandemic, believing businesses were putting profits before people and doing a poor job of protecting workers. Only 29 percent of those surveyed believed business leaders were doing an "outstanding" job of handling the crisis.[156] As Edelman CEO Richard Edelman remarked, "The speed and scale of the lockdowns, the brave

---

153 "An Evaluation of the Paycheck Protection Program Using Administrative Payroll Microdata," Report (Cambridge, Massachusetts: Massachusetts Institute of Technology, 2020).

154 Ibid.

155 Lucy Handley, "Trust in Governments Surges during Pandemic but People Are Disappointed with CEO Performance," CNBC, May 5, 2020.

156 Ibid.

performance of the public health services and the extent of public expenditure to support the private sector have shown government taking quick decisive action. This is a stunning turnaround for government, which has always languished at or near the bottom of the trust hierarchy."[157]

At the beginning of 2020, business and the private sectors were portrayed as greater and more effective change-makers than government. People were wondering what the role of government even was anymore in society. The private sector could fix all the problems society was facing and do it with less money. And then COVID-19 hit. People realized there are some things business can't do and government has to do. The state and federal government can order lockdowns for public health; businesses can't. Government can distribute industry bailouts and unemployment benefits; businesses can't. Government can subsidize and ensure a speedy production of vaccines; businesses can't. Public servants are the superheroes of the coronavirus pandemic. As Liliana Mason put it, "It is no longer 'terrifying' to hear the words 'I'm from the government, and I'm here to help.'" In fact, that's what most people are desperately hoping to hear right now. We will see a rebirth of the patriotic honor of working for the government."[158]

In the present day, it's hard to imagine a renaissance of public service; at best, it seems bold, at worst, dangerously naive. How can I say that I believe more young people will enter

---

157 Ibid.
158 Lilliana Mason, "Coronavirus Will Change the World Permanently. Here's How," *POLITICO Magazine*, April 15, 2020.

government after this pandemic considering the numbers pre-pandemic?

Because of this country's history.

At every inflection point in US history, Americans have risen up and met the call of public service. From the Civil War, to World War II, to the attacks on 9/11, Americans have rallied at every crisis point. COVID-19 is no exception. Already, millions of people have acted in concert to stem the proliferation of this disease. And as this crisis continues, I believe public service will only strengthen, not falter.

Furthermore, Americans—especially young Americans—have always made their voices heard in times of government failure or inaction. Whether it be protesting against the Vietnam War or for civil rights or climate change, young people have always responded to injustice not with defeat, but with heightened urgency. The failure of the federal government to respond to the COVID-19 pandemic will inspire the next generation of public servants. In the face of failure, young people have always dared to dream for a better country, a better world.

CONCLUSION

———

A few weeks ago, I had dinner with a good friend, Svy, who I had met during my semester in Washington, DC. Svy and I share many of the same interests and beliefs. We both love debating politics and foreign policy, and, most importantly, love a good brunch with friends. But we fundamentally differ in our approaches to our post-grad prospects. I'm a little (a lot) more frenzied, spending too many days writing cover letters, applying for internships, and stressing over every interview. Svy is much more deliberate. Maybe it's the wisdom of being a year older than me, but Svy doesn't stress over minutiae. It's a skill I haven't yet mastered.

At dinner one evening, I asked Svy about what full-time positions he was applying for. He was a senior, graduating in less than nine months. The question made sense, and I was looking for examples of what to pursue as I became a senior as well. But Svy's response surprised me. "I'm not sure yet. I want to apply for the Peace Corps, but I'm also thinking about other things as well. I wouldn't mind taking a year to do something completely random and think about what I want to really pursue in life."

That may not seem like a revolutionary answer. Svy seems like a regular college student trying to figure out his next steps. What struck me as extraordinarily remarkable, though, was the fact that Svy said it with such ease. He was comfortable with the uncertainty of it all. Comfort in uncertainty is a rarity in the world I inhabit. Most of my peers are intelligent beyond belief, fiercely driven, and extremely confident on the surface. But deep down is an underlying current of fear—fear of risk, of failure, of the unknown. That's why most of my peers choose internships and jobs that guarantee a pathway to success—investment banking, management consulting, medical school, law school. Most are trying to avoid the unknown.

Svy is one of the few people I know who has embraced the unknown. It's not that he's directionless. His goal is to attend graduate school to get a master's degree in international relations and eventually join the State Department as a Foreign Service Officer. Service is important to Svy as well. He's just not in a rush.

During my few years in college, writing this book, and talking to hundreds of great people like Svy, I've realized it takes time to pinpoint what you're passionate about and how you want to make a difference in the world. But most of us don't take the time to do so. Why? Well, part of that is external pressure. The world, especially in the social media era, moves rapidly. People worry they'll get left behind, so they commit to jobs, careers, and lifestyles before they're ready to. I see it all the time in college; the pressure from friends, peers, and family members forces many students to choose a job without exploring what they want to pursue in life. Sadly, the external pressure doesn't stop once you graduate college either; it only gets worse as you grow older.

Part of why we don't stop and take the time to discover what we want to pursue in life is also internal. It's the fear of uncertainty; the fear we'll discover that the path we'd been heading down was the wrong one; the fear that the new path is much more unsure and unexplored than the one on which we originally started. But the people who take the time to think about what they truly want out of their lives are infinitely happier and more fulfilled.

This pressure, both external and internal, is where public service gets short-changed.

To be clear, public service isn't every person's destiny in life, and that's completely okay. But so many people, especially students, will never know if public service is for them because the other options are simply easier to find. The rushed recruitment techniques of the private sector prevent students from fully considering the public sector. Some students commit to their full-time jobs by the spring of their sophomore year. A person's nineteen-year-old self might not want the same things as their twenty-three-year-old self. No longer is college the time for exploration and purposeful uncertainty but, rather, a time of stress and premature commitment.

Some students may know public service is for them from day one of high school or college, but for the rest, it may take longer. It may take asking difficult questions and going through periods of uncertainty and exploration. It may take years of self-discovery and mistakes and false starts. It's an arduous, emotionally draining process, but ultimately, most people I've talked to who have gone through it—who have asked the hard questions and ended up in the public sector—hold no regrets. And to me, that's been infinitely inspiring.

Throughout this book, I've tried to tackle one singular problem: why so few young people work in the public sector. It turns out, that singular problem encompasses multitudes.

I previously said the issue isn't demand, and that has held true throughout. Gen Zers want to work for government. Unlike their millennial older siblings, who gravitated toward the idea of working for good through the private sector rather than government, Gen Z approaches the idea of social good differently. Private sector companies once branded "do-gooders," like Facebook and Google, have recently come under fire for harmful antitrust and privacy issues. Seismic events like the COVID-19 pandemic and the Black Lives Matter movement have fundamentally transformed the Gen Z mentality. Gen Zers want to effect change through government—through an expanded governmental mandate—rather than through the private sector.

Gen Zers just don't know where the opportunities are. Governmental agencies fail to properly utilize campus recruiting and fail to develop necessary relationships with university career centers. The public sector does an even worse job recruiting students from historically marginalized and underrepresented groups. Students like Hillary Shah, who go to state schools that are often overlooked by the public sector, are eager to work in government. They just don't know where to look.

Even when Gen Zers find public sector opportunities, the barriers to entry are too high or the onboarding process is too long, prompting many people to drop out of it altogether. Think about Amy, the public health officer who had to wait over two years to be accepted into the Commissioned Corps of the US Public Service, or Sophie, who applied through a streamlined program and still had to wait three months to begin her job. Most people can't or won't wait that long to start their careers.

The good news is that these problems are solvable. First, we can create sustainable public sector pipelines that appeal to Gen Z. The public sector can learn from leaders like Reed Shafer-Ray, cofounder of Lead for America, who has successfully recruited cohorts of recent college graduates to work in local government for two years. Reed didn't have a recruiting budget; he recruited by developing relationships with potential candidates and fostering personal relationships.

Second, the government can expand the role of civic tech. Tech-savvy young people want to work for a purpose; government can fill that role. In addition, we can learn from the lessons of civic tech by hiring based on skills rather than experience, streamlining the federal hiring process, and creating agile work teams.

Finally, we can lean into the momentum created by the COVID-19 pandemic. The government's role in the day-to-day lives of ordinary Americans has never been greater. But more importantly, people remember what it means to serve. Post-pandemic, people will want to continue to serve and make a difference in their communities.

I won't say these problems are easy to solve or won't require a huge investment of time and money. They will. But we need to fix them for the sake of our country.

I wrote this book in the year 2020, as the country seemingly burned to the ground. The year wasn't a good one for the world, for the United States, or for our government. We all experienced a global pandemic, a contentious presidential election, and heightened levels of partisanship not seen since the Civil War. And yet, I came out of 2020 more optimistic than I entered it. Why? Because while our government was being pinned down and fighting one challenge after another, I was interviewing the people holding the country up—the civil servant fighting for racial equality; the public health officer fighting COVID-19 in populations forgotten to the rest of the world; the technologist who could be making millions of dollars at a Big Tech firm but, instead, was using their skills to make health care accessible to all veterans.

I almost feel as if everyone should be required to write a book about the American government and talk to the people who work for it because these people are *great*. They're kind, they're passionate, and they're duty driven. We need more of these people in government, and Gen Z is eager to take on the challenges of both the present and the future. The public sector just needs to invest in their potential workforce of the future.

I hope by reading this book, you've gotten a glimpse of the great people who serve our country. I hope you've become more optimistic about the direction of our country as well. Change and better days will come because of the people fighting for that change. That, I know for sure.

ACKNOWLEDGEMENTS

I am profoundly grateful to my editors, friends, teachers, and family members for making this book happen.

Thank you to my editors, Avery Lockland and Bianca Myrtil, for your insightful edits and unyielding patience. This book is infinitely better thanks to both of you. Thank you also to Eric Koester, Brian Bies, and everyone on the New Degrees Press team for making this book what it is.

Special thank you to my amazing friends who told me I could write a book even before I believed it myself. Thank you to my high school friends—Lucy Liu, Adele Harshbarger, Manon Veltman, Caroline Mullooly, and Nora Murphy—for the endless laughs and unwavering support. Thank you to my Penn friends—Alyssa Lu, Quinn Gallagher, Linda Wang, Armaan Tobaccowalla, and Danielle Lo—for the Four Yellow Table memories and late-night dinners. And thank you to my Penn in Washington cohort (especially Svyatoslav Karnasevych, Eva Gonzales, Tara Yazdan Panah, and Ammar Lone) for inspiring me with your passion for public service and dedication to social change. A big thanks to James Nycz for believing in this project and taking the time to meticulously edit my manuscript.

In addition, I would like to thank my high school teachers and college professors for instilling my love of learning. Thank you to Mr. Peter Gouveia, Mr. George Krajca, Mr. Kevin Kelly, and Ms. Kristen Warner for inspiring my love of writing and government. To Professor Amanda Shanor and Professor Brian Berkey, thank you for all of your academic and career advice. And I want to especially thank Dr. Stephen Epstein for supporting this crazy idea before I had written a single word.

Finally, I would like to thank my family for their unconditional love and support. Thanks to Auntie Manju, Grandma, Gong Gong, Po Po, Sabrina Yam, Andrew Yam, and Uncle Willie for always being there for me. Thanks to my brother, Zach, for being a creative, kind, intelligent person—I can't wait for you to join me at Penn. Lastly, this book is dedicated to my parents who have always believed in me and encouraged me to pursue my passions.

I would also like to acknowledge everyone who supported this book:

Cathy DuRei, Syamala Jonnalagadda, Peter Suranyi, Armaan Tobaccowalla, Talia Statsky-Frank, Eva Gonzalez, Lisette Garza, Jeff Lightfield, Angelo Del Priore, Carlos Soto, Svyatoslav Karnasevych, Lauren King, Sita Rentala, Sabrina Yam, Jason & Julie Hammerman, Nancy Chew, Donaya Luangchotikul, Nora Murphy, Thomas Kibarian, Linda Lew, Cathleen Colvin, Sorcha McCrohan, Justin Taylor Lieb, Duytam

Vu, David Thai, Keren Stearns, Yuko Watanabe, Kathryn Kelly Massa, Munir Alam, Lynn T Cetin, Kahleen Rozowsky, Heather Cabot Khemlani, Ann Parkin, Rodney A. Brown, Veronica Zamora-Campos, Diane Keenley, Neha Bar, Donna B. McElwee, Gabriela M. Stout, Katherine Montrone, Kamal Ardeshna, Barbara Williams, Stephanie Delurgio, Nicole Hazard, Adam Fine, Eric Koester, Joseph Vangala, Willie Yam, Melinda Hu, Quinn Gallagher, Olivia O'Dwyer, Jesse Cui, Sophia Tareen, William Snow, Aliris Tang, Adele Harshbarger, Caroline Mullooly, Vivian Dai, Isaac Lee, Sara Brizio, Chase Dexter, Maya Nachman, Margaret Cheng, Michael Nevett, Alicia Lu, Mika Mizobuchi, Hima Kher, Sunny Sousa, Sophia Ye, Manju Rentala, Aliyah Rose, Joey Lohmann, Peter Gouveia, Lucy Liu, Jason Xiao, Valerie De Cruz, Danielle Lo, Linda Wang, James Nycz, Alyssa Lu, Tara Yazdan Panah, Kamilla Yunosova, Peyton Walters, and Cindy Rentala

APPENDIX

INTRODUCTION

Buchanan, Larry, Quoctrung Bui, Jugal K. Patel. "Black Lives Matter May Be the Largest Movement in US History." *New York Times*, July 3, 2020. https://www.nytimes.com/interactive/2020/07/03/us/george-floyd-protests-crowd-size.html.

Cohen, Li. "From TikTok to Black Lives Matter, how Gen Z is Revolutionizing Activism." *CBS News*, July 20, 2020. https://www.cbsnews.com/news/from-tiktok-to-black-lives-matter-how-gen-z-is-revolutionizing-activism/.

Corrigan, Jack. "At One Civilian Agency, IT Pros over 60 Years Old Outnumber Their under 30 Colleagues 19 to One." *Nextgov*, October 01, 2018. https://www.nextgov.com/cio-briefing/2018/10/numbers-federal-agencies-struggle-hiring-young-techies/151669/.

Corrigan, Jack. "The Hollowing-Out of the State Department Continues." *The Atlantic*, February 11, 2018. https://www.theatlantic.

com/international/archive/2018/02/tillerson-trump-state-foreign-service/553034/.

Cournoyer, Caroline. "Generation Z Wants a Job. Are You Ready to Hire Them?" *Governing*, March 23, 2017. https://www.governing.com/archive/gov-generation-z-workforce.html.

De Luce, Dan. "Fewer Americans Are Opting for Careers at the State Department." *NBC News*, February 25, 2019. https://www.nbcnews.com/politics/national-security/fewer-americans-are-opting-careers-state-department-n973631.

Hensch, Mark. "A Quarter of Feds Plans on Retiring Within 25 Years." *Govloop*, October 30, 2018. https://www.govloop.com/25-percent-of-feds-plan-on-retiring-within-5-years/.

Neal, Jeff. "Government Hiring of Young People Continues to Be Terrible." Federal News Network, May 1, 2019. https://federalnewsnetwork.com/commentary/2019/05/government-hiring-of-young-people-continues-to-be-terrible/.

Smith, Ben. "Obama Plans To 'Make Government Cool Again." *Politico*, September 11, 2008. https://www.politico.com/blogs/ben-smith/2008/09/obama-plans-to-make-government-cool-again-011772.

Tankersley, Jim, Margot Sanger-Katz, Alan Rappeport, Emily Cochrane. "Trump's $4.8 Trillion Budget Would Cut Safety Net Programs and Boost Defense." *New York Times*, February 10, 2020. https://www.nytimes.com/2020/02/10/business/president-trump-budget-cuts.html.

US News and World Report. "High Technology High School."
Accessed September 04, 2020. https://www.usnews.com/
education/best-high-schools/new-jersey/districts/mon-
mouth-county-vocational-school-district/high-technology-
high-school-12808.

Vinik, Danny. "America's Government is Getting Old." *Politico*, September 27, 2017. https://www.politico.com/agenda/
story/2017/09/27/aging-government-workforce-analy-
sis-000525/.

CHAPTER ONE

"Carly Fiorina Fast Facts." CNN. updated June 26, 2020, accessed
September 11, 2020. https://www.cnn.com/2015/05/28/us/car-
ly-fiorina-fast-facts/index.html.

"For Millennials It's Not Just the Money That Counts." Morgan
Stanley. Accessed September 04, 2020. https://www.morgan-
stanley.com/articles/volunteering-opportunities-are-attract-
ing-millennials-to-banking.

Forsythe, Michael. "When Pete Buttigieg Was One of McKinsey's
'Whiz Kids.'" *New York Times,* December 10, 2019. https://www.
nytimes.com/2019/12/05/us/politics/pete-buttigieg-mckinsey.
html.

Giridharadas, Anand. *Winners Take All: The Elite Charade of
Changing the World.* New York: Knopf, 2018.

Ho, Catherine. "Romney Suggests Business Experience Should
Be Prerequisite to Presidency." *The Washington Post,* June 3,

2012. https://www.washingtonpost.com/business/capitalbusiness/romney-suggests-business-experience-should-be-prerequisite-to-presidency/2012/06/01/gJQATmp7BV_story.html.

Klar, Rebecca. "Steyer Touts Business Experience in Economic Address." *The Hill*, December 16, 2019. https://thehill.com/homenews/campaign/474679-steyer-touts-business-experience-in-economic-address.

Kramer, Curtlyn. "Vital Stats: The Growing Influence of Businesspeople in Congress." *Brookings Institution*, February 17, 2017. https://www.brookings.edu/blog/fixgov/2017/02/17/vital-stats-businesspeople-in-congress/.

McGrath, Ben. "The Untouchable." *The New Yorker*, August 17, 2009. https://www.newyorker.com/magazine/2009/08/24/the-untouchable.

Murray, Seb. "Even McKinsey, Bain, BCG Are Offering MBAs Social Impact Consulting Careers." *Business Because*, February 25, 2016. https://www.businessbecause.com/news/mba-jobs/3813/mckinsey-bain-bcg-offer-social-impact-careers.

"Philanthropy." McKinsey. Accessed September 04, 2020. https://www.mckinsey.com/industries/public-and-social-sector/how-we-help-clients/philanthropy.

Simpson, Connor. "Mitt Romney Makes His Bain Defense in Wall Street Journal Editorial." *The Atlantic*, August 23, 2012. https://www.theatlantic.com/politics/archive/2012/08/mitt-romney-makes-his-bain-defense-wall-street-journal-editorial/324342/.

"Social Impact." Bain. Accessed September 04, 2020. https://www.bain.com/about/social-impact/.

"Top 10 Reasons to Join Deloitte." Deloitte. Accessed September 04, 2020. https://www2.deloitte.com/us/en/pages/careers/articles/about-deloitte-careers-top-ten-reasons-to-join-deloitte.html.

"We Are the Centre for Public Impact." Boston Consulting Group. Accessed September 04, 2020. https://www.centreforpublicimpact.org/about-us/.

Yang, Andrew. "When people ask if I'm surprised by the success of our campaign, I remind them that I have founded and run multi-million-dollar organizations that began with just an idea. This feels very familiar. And we are not done yet." Twitter, November 11, 2019. https://twitter.com/andrewyang/status/1193977585803431937?lang=en.

CHAPTER TWO

Brinkley, Joel. "Reagan Appoints Privatization Unit." *New York Times*, September 04, 1987. https://www.nytimes.com/1987/09/04/us/reagan-appoints-privatization-unit.html.

Brownstein, Ronald. "The Race Unifying Boomers and Gen Z." *The Atlantic*, June 18, 2020. https://www.theatlantic.com/politics/archive/2020/06/todays-protest-movements-are-as-big-as-the-1960s/613207/.

Davis, Dominic-Madori. "The Action Generation: How Gen Z Really Feels about Race, Equality, and Its Role in the Historic George Floyd Protests, Based on a Survey of 39,000 Young

Americans." *Business Insider*, June 10, 2020. https://www.
businessinsider.com/how-gen-z-feels-about-george-floyd-
protests-2020-6.

Gergen, David and Caroline Cohen. "The Next Greatest Generation." *CNN*, June 14, 2020. https://www.cnn.com/2020/06/14/
opinions/black-lives-matter-gen-z-greatest-generation-gergen-
cohen/index.html.

Goodman, B. John and Gary W. Loveman. "Does Privatization
Serve the Public Interest?" *Harvard Business Review*, November-December 1991. https://hbr.org/1991/11/does-privatiza-
tion-serve-the-public-interest.

Google. "Our Approach to Search." Google Search. Accessed September 07, 2020. https://www.google.com/search/howsearch-
works/mission/.

Laughlin, Nick. "How 2020 is Impacting Gen Z's Worldview." *Morning Consult*, July 6, 2020. https://morningconsult.
com/form/gen-z-worldview-tracker/.

Limbachia, Dixie. "Mark Zuckerberg Unveils Facebook's New
Mission Statement." *Variety*, June 22, 2017. https://variety.
com/2017/digital/news/mark-zuckerberg-changes-face-
book-mission-1202476176/.

Mazzucato, Mariana. *The Entrepreneurial State: Debunking Public
vs. Private Sector Myths.* London: Anthem Press, 2013.

Nelson, Angela. "Young Voters Were Crucial to Biden's Win." *Tufts-Now*, November 12, 2020. https://now.tufts.edu/articles/young-voters-were-crucial-to-biden-s-win.

Ning, Alan. "Saving VA $100 Million Dollars." *US Digital Service* (blog), April 20, 2018. https://medium.com/the-u-s-digital-service/saving-va-100-million-dollars-c5d992e0cf54.

Parker, Kim and Ruth Igielnik. "On the Cusp of Adulthood and Facing an Uncertain Future: What We Know About Gen Z So Far." *Pew Research Center*, May 14, 2020. https://www.pewsocialtrends.org/essay/on-the-cusp-of-adulthood-and-facing-an-uncertain-future-what-we-know-about-gen-z-so-far/.

Perrigo, Billy. "The World Wide Web Turns 30 Today. Here's How Its Inventor Thinks We Can Fix It." *Time Magazine*, March 12, 2019. time.com/5549635/tim-berners-lee-interview-web/.

Seymour, Emily. "Gen Z: Studies Show Higher Rates of Depression." VOA News, August 25, 2019. https://www.voanews.com/student-union/gen-z-studies-show-higher-rates-depression.

CHAPTER 3

Brown. Fallon Susan. "Four Traps in Federal Recruiting, and How to Avoid Them." *Government Executive*, October 31, 2018. https://www.govexec.com/management/2018/10/four-traps-federal-recruiting-and-how-avoid-them/152441/.

College Students Are Attracted to Federal Service, but Agencies Need to Capitalize on Their Interest. Washington DC: Partnership for Public Service and National Association of College and

Employees, 2014. Accessed August 29, 2020. https://ourpub-licservice.org/wp-content/uploads/2014/03/08cfe7a90149145f-2e0f90a564ae1402-1396883817.pdf.

Durak, Dan and Wendy Ginsberg. "Government's Lack of Diversity in Leadership Positions." *Partnership for Public Service,* March 11, 2019. https://ourpublicservice.org/blog-governments-lack-of-diversity-in-leadership-positions/.

Peters, Anna. "Recruitment Strategies for Government Agencies to Quickly Hire Students and Grads at Scale." *College Recruiter,* March 29, 2018. https://www.collegerecruiter.com/blog/2018/03/29/innovative-recruiting-strategies-for-government-agencies-to-quickly-hire-dozens-or-hundreds-of-students-and-recent-grads/.

CHAPTER 4

Grundmann, Tsui Susan. "The Impact of Recruitment Strategy on Fair and Open Competition for Federal Jobs." *A Report to the President and the Congress of the United States by the US Merit Systems Protection Board.* Washington, DC: US Merit Systems Protection Board, 2015. Accessed September 18, 2020. https://www.mspb.gov/netsearch/viewdocs.aspx-?docnumber=1118751&version=1123213&application=ACRO-BAT.

Indeed. "How to Build a Federal Resume (With Template)." Career Guide. Accessed September 11, 2020. https://www.indeed.com/career-advice/resumes-cover-letters/federal-resume-template.

Nyczepir, Dave. "USDS Wants to Fix the 'Black Hole; USAJOBS With Alternative Hiring Assessment." *FedScoop*, October 23, 2019. https://www.fedscoop.com/usds-it-hiring-hhs-nps/.

OPM. "Policy, Data, Oversight." Hiring Information. Accessed September 18, 2020. https://www.opm.gov/policy-data-oversight/hiring-information/students-recent-graduates/.

Roberts, Michael. "10 Steps in the Government Hiring Process." *The Balance Careers*, June 25, 2019. https://www.thebalancecareers. com/steps-in-the-government-hiring-process-1669545.

CHAPTER FIVE

Alexander, Reed. "From Goldman Sachs to Morgan Stanley, Here's What Bulge-Bracket Banks are Paying Their First-Year IB Analysts." *Business Insider*, August 24, 2020. https://www.businessinsider.com/salaries-first-year-investment-banking-analysts-make-2020-8.

Berman, Jillian. "The Trump Administration Proposes Eliminating Public Service Loan Forgiveness." *MarketWatch*, March 12, 2019. https://www.marketwatch.com/story/the-trump-administration-proposes-eliminating-public-service-loan-forgiveness-2019-03-12?mod=article_inline.

Chermerinsky, Making Sense of the Affirmative Action Debate, 22 Ohio N.U. Law Review. 1343 (1996).

"Comparing the Compensation of Federal and Private sector Employees, 2011 to 2015." Report. Washington, DC: Congres-

sional Budget Office, 2017. Accessed August 26, 2020. https://
www.cbo.gov/publication/52637.

Douglas-Gabriel, Danielle. "Education Dept. Rejects Vast Majority of Applicants for Temporary Student Loan Forgiveness
Program." *Washington Post*, April 2, 2019. https://www.
washingtonpost.com/education/2019/04/03/education-dept-
rejects-vast-majority-applicants-temporary-student-loan-
forgiveness-program/.

Federal Pay. "Executive & Senior Level Employees Pay Tables."
Accessed August 27, 2020. https://www.federalpay.org/ses/2020.

Federal Student Aid. "Public Service Loan Forgiveness Data."
Accessed August 27, 2020. https://studentaid.gov/data-center/
student/loan-forgiveness/pslf-data.

General Schedule. "How Much Does a GS-15 Employee Get Paid?"
Accessed August 27, 2020. https://www.generalschedule.org/
GS-15.

Go Government. "Glossary." Accessed August 27, 2020. https://
gogovernment.org/about/glossary/.

Go Government. "Pay and the General Schedule (GS)." Accessed
August 27, 2020. https://gogovernment.org/pay-and-the-gen-
eral-schedule-gs/.

Jones, James R. "The Color of Congress: Racial Representation
Among Interns in the US House of Representatives." *Report.*
Washington, DC: Pay Our Interns, 2016. Accessed August 26,
2020. https://payourinterns.org/congressional-report.

Leswing, Kig. "Here's How Big Tech Companies Like Google and Facebook Set Salaries for Software Engineers." *CNBC,* June 16, 2019. https://www.cnbc.com/2019/06/14/how-much-google-facebook-other-tech-giants-pay-software-engineers.html.

Management Consulted. "Management Consultant Salary." Accessed February 9, 2021. https://managementconsulted.com/consultant-salary/.

Markovits, Daniel. *The Meritocracy Trap: How America's Foundational Myth Feeds Inequality, Dismantles the Middle Class, and Devours the Elite.* New York: Penguin Press, 2019.

Mikovich, T. George, Alexander Wigdor, Renae Broderick, Anne Mavor. "Pay for Performance." *A Report Evaluating Performance Appraisal and Merit Pay.* Washington, DC: Commission on Behavioral and Social Sciences and Education, 1991. Accessed August 26, 2020. https://www.nap.edu/read/1751/chapter/4.

United States Senator from Virginia. "Gillibrand, Kaine Lead Group Of 13 Senators to Introduce New Legislation to Overhaul Flawed Public Service Loan Forgiveness Program, Ensure Millions of Americans Will Now Be Eligible for the Loan Forgiveness They Have Earned." Press release, April 11, 2019. Website. https://www.kaine.senate.gov/press-releases/gillibrand-kaine-lead-group-of-13-senators-to-introduce-new-legislation-to-overhaul-flawed-public-service-loan-forgiveness-program-ensure-millions-of-americans-will-now-be-eligible-for-the-loan-forgiveness-they-have-earned accessed August 27, 2020.

USA Facts. "College Tuition Has Increased—But What's the Actual Cost?" Accessed August 27, 2020. https://usafacts.org/articles/college-tuition-has-increased-but-whats-the-actual-cost/.

Weiss, Cassens Debra. "Public Service Workers Denied Loan Forgiveness Due to Wrong Repayment Plan Given Second Chance." *ABA Journal*, May 30, 2018. https://www.abajournal.com/news/article/public_service_workers_denied_loan_forgiveness_due_to_wrong_repayment_plan/.

Wilson, Martha. "The Ugly Truth About Promotions." *FedSmith*, January 19, 2015. https://www.fedsmith.com/2015/01/19/the-ugly-truth-about-promotions/.

CHAPTER SIX

Biden Harris. "The Biden Plan for Education Beyond High School." Accessed September 30, 2020. https://joebiden.com/beyondhs/.

DeFelice, Manon. "What Gen Z Wants at Work Will Blow Your Mind." *Forbes*, October 31, 2019. https://www.forbes.com/sites/manondefelice/2019/10/31/what-gen-z-wants-at-work-will-blow-your-mind/.

Falk, Justin. "Comparing the Compensation of Federal and Private sector Employees, 2011 to 2015." *Report*. Washington, DC: Congressional Budget Office, 2017. Accessed September 30, 2020. https://www.cbo.gov/publication/52637.

Miller, Josh. "A 16-Year-Old Explains 10 Things You Need to Know About Generation Z." *Society for Human Resource Management*, October 30, 2018. https://www.shrm.org/hr-today/news/

hr-magazine/1118/pages/a-16-year-old-explains-10-things-you-need-to-know-about-generation-z.aspx.

Millsap, Adam. "Upskilling Workers for the Post-Pandemic Economy." *Forbes*, September 4, 2020. https://www.forbes.com/sites/adammillsap/2020/09/04/upskilling-workers-for-the-post-pandemic-economy/.

PR Newswire. "Survey: Student Loan Debt Is a Key Factor for Gen Z When Making Career Decisions." Accessed September 30, 2020. https://www.prnewswire.com/news-releases/survey-student-loan-debt-is-a-key-factor-for-gen-z-when-making-career-decisions-300991206.html.

"Retirement Security Across Generations." Report. Washington, DC: Pew Charitable Trust, 2013. Accessed September 30, 2020. from https://www.pewtrusts.org/en/research-and-analysis/reports/0001/01/01/retirement-security-across-generations.

Sears, Hannah. "Why Mission-Driven Brands are Winning in 2019." *Pixlee* (blog), April 22, 2019. https://www.pixlee.com/blog/why-mission-driven-brands-are-winning-in-2019/.

Shafer-Ray, Reed. "The Tragedy of Selling Out: Trading Civic Aspirations for Six Figures." *The Harvard Crimson*, November 9, 2017. https://www.thecrimson.com/column/trans4mations/article/2017/11/9/shafer-ray-the-tragedy-of-selling-out/.

"The Pathways Programs: Their Use and Effectiveness Two Years After Implementation." Special Study. Washington, DC: US Office of Personnel Management, 2016. Accessed January 20, 2021. https://www.opm.gov/policy-data-oversight/hiring-in-

formation/students-recent-graduates/reference-materials/
report-on-special-study-of-the-pathways-programs.pdf.

United States Senator from Virginia. "Gillibrand, Kaine Lead
Group Of 13 Senators to Introduce New Legislation to Overhaul Flawed Public Service Loan Forgiveness Program,
Ensure Millions of Americans Will Now Be Eligible for the
Loan Forgiveness They Have Earned." Press release, April 11,
2019. Website. https://www.kaine.senate.gov/press-releases/
gillibrand-kaine-lead-group-of-13-senators-to-introduce-
new-legislation-to-overhaul-flawed-public-service-loan-for-
giveness-program-ensure-millions-of-americans-will-now-be-
eligible-for-the-loan-forgiveness-they-have-earned accessed
August 27, 2020.

CHAPTER 7

About. "Who We Are." Presidential Innovation Fellows, accessed
September 25, 2020. https://presidentialinnovationfellows.gov/
about/.

"Building a New Field of Public Interest Technology: Lessons
Learned from Public Interest Law." Research Report. Washington, DC: Ford Foundation, 2018. Accessed September 27, 2020.
https://www.fordfoundation.org/work/learning/research-re-
ports/building-a-new-field-of-public-interest-technology-les-
sons-learned-from-public-interest-law/.

Chappellet-Lanier, Tajha. "The White House Wants to Make Civic
Leave for Technologists Normal and Accessible. Will it Take
Off?" *FedScoop*, October 24, 2018. https://www.fedscoop.com/
civic-leave-white-house-technology-company-employees/.

Coding it Forward. "Our Story." Accessed September 27, 2020. https://www.codingitforward.com/about.

"Corporate Civic Responsibility: A New Paradigm for Companies to Advance Public Interest Technology." Report. Washington, DC: Ford Foundation and Tech Talent Project, 2020. https://techtalentproject.org/wp-content/uploads/2021/01/Corporate-Civic-Responsibility_Chan_TechTalentProject_1.6.21.pdf.

Fretwell, Luke. "A Brief History of Open Data." *FCW*, June 9, 2014. https://fcw.com/articles/2014/06/09/exec-tech-brief-history-of-open-data.aspx.

Goldstein, Amy. "HHS Failed to Heed Many Warnings That HealthCare.gov Was in Trouble." *Washington Post*, February 23, 2016. https://www.washingtonpost.com/national/health-science/hhs-failed-to-heed-many-warnings-that-healthcaregov-was-in-trouble/2016/02/22/dd344e7c-d67e-11e5-9823-02b905009f99_story.html.

Goldstein, Amy and Juliet Eilperin. "HealthCare.gov: How Political Fear Was Pitted Against Technical Needs." *Washington Post*, November 2, 2013. https://www.washingtonpost.com/politics/challenges-have-dogged-obamas-health-plan-since-2010/2013/11/02/453fba42-426b-11e3-a624-41d661b0bb78_story.html.

Hochmuth, Colby. "US CTO Stepping Down." *FCW*, August 22, 2014. https://fcw.com/articles/2014/08/22/todd-park-resigns.aspx.

[Levy, Steven. "The Final Days of Obama's Tech Surge." *Wired*, January 10, 2017. https://www.wired.com/2017/01/the-final-days-of-obamas-tech-surge/.

Nisen, Max. "A 64-year-old Engineer is Suing Google for Age Discrimination." *Quartz*, April 24, 2015. https://qz.com/390835/google-age-discrimination/.

Ogrysko, Nicole. "2020 is the Year for Scaling Up Trump Administration Workforce Pilots." Federal News Network, January 9, 2020. https://federalnewsnetwork.com/workforce/2020/01/2020-is-the-year-for-scaling-up-trump-administration-workforce-pilots/.

Ogrysko, Nicole. "Agencies Find Higher Quality Candidates Under New Digital Service, OPM Hiring Pilot." Federal News Network, October 25, 2019. https://federalnewsnetwork.com/hiring-retention/2019/10/agencies-find-higher-quality-candidates-under-new-digital-service-opm-hiring-pilot/.

Our Story. "Our First Tech President." Obama Foundation, accessed September 25, 2020. https://www.obama.org/chapter/our-first-tech-president/.

Owens, Simon. "Can Todd Park Revolutionize the Health Care Industry?" *The Atlantic*, June 2, 2011. https://www.theatlantic.com/technology/archive/2011/06/can-todd-park-revolutionize-the-health-care-industry/239708/.

Public Interest Tech. "Individuals." Ford Foundation. Accessed September 27, 2020. https://www.fordfoundation.org/campaigns/public-interest-tech/individuals/.

Prang, Allison. "Athenahealth to Sell Itself for $5.47 Billion." *Wall Street Journal*, November 12, 2018. https://www.wsj.com/articles/athenahealth-to-sell-itself-for-5-47-billion-1542035482.

Quora. "What Is Civic Technology?" *Forbes*, September 19, 2017. https://www.forbes.com/sites/quora/2017/09/19/what-is-civic-technology/.

Sinai, Nick. "Congress Should Grow the Digital Services Budget, Which More Than Pays for Itself." *The Hill*, May 17, 2019. https://thehill.com/opinion/technology/444159-congress-should-grow-the-digital-services-budget-which-more-than-pays-for.

TechCongress. "About Us." Accessed September 27, 2020. https://www.techcongress.io/about-us.

Thorp, Frank. "Only 6 Able to Sign Up on Healthcare.gov's First Day, Documents Show." *NBC News*, October 31, 2013. https://www.nbcnews.com/news/other/only-6-able-sign-healthcare-govs-first-day-documents-show-f8C11509571.

US Digital Service. "How We Work." Accessed September 26, 2020. https://www.usds.gov/how-we-work.

CHAPTER EIGHT

"Americans' Views of Government: Low Trust, but Some Positive Performance Ratings." Pew Research Center, September 14, 2020. Accessed October 9, 2020. https://www.pewresearch.org/politics/2020/09/14/americans-views-of-government-low-trust-but-some-positive-performance-ratings/.

"An Evaluation of the Paycheck Protection Program Using Administrative Payroll Microdata." Report. Cambridge, Massachusetts: Massachusetts Institute of Technology, 2020. http://economics.mit.edu/files/20094.

Graham, W. Daniel. "Heraclitus." *Stanford Encyclopedia of Philosophy*, September 3, 2019. https://plato.stanford.edu/entries/heraclitus/.

Handley, Lucy. "Trust in Governments Surges during Pandemic but People Are Disappointed with CEO Performance." CNBC, May 5, 2020. https://www.cnbc.com/2020/05/05/trust-in-governments-increases-during-pandemic-but-ceos-disappoint.html.

Kakutani, Michiko. "Coronavirus Will Change the World Permanently. Here's How." *POLITICO Magazine*, April 15, 2020. https://www.politico.com/news/magazine/2020/03/19/coronavirus-effect-economy-life-society-analysis-covid-135579.

Mason, Liliana. "Coronavirus Will Change the World Permanently. Here's How." *POLITICO Magazine*, April 15, 2020. https://www.politico.com/news/magazine/2020/03/19/coronavirus-effect-economy-life-society-analysis-covid-135579.

"Samantha Power: Change what Seems Possible." *Lehigh News*, October 24, 2018. Accessed October 9, 2020. https://www2.lehigh.edu/news/samantha-power-change-what-seems-possible.

Semones, Evan. "'Wrong!': Trump Slams Fauci over Testimony on Covid-19 Surge." *POLITICO Magazine*, August 1, 2020. https://

www.politico.com/news/2020/08/01/wrong-trump-rebukes-fauci-in-tweet-390150.

Tavernise, Sabrina. "Will the Coronavirus Kill What's Left of Americans' Faith in Washington?" *The New York Times*, May 23, 2020. https://www.nytimes.com/2020/05/23/us/coronavirus-government-trust.html.

Weiner, Mark. "Digital Views for Cuomo's Daily Coronavirus Briefings Set Records." Syracuse.com, March 31, 2020. https://www.syracuse.com/coronavirus/2020/03/digital-views-for-cuomos-daily-coronavirus-briefings-near-1m-a-day.html.

Whoriskey, Peter and Douglas MacMillan. "'Doomed to Fail': Why a $4 Trillion Bailout Couldn't Revive the American Economy." *The Washington Post*, October 5, 2020.

#Peter Whoriskey, Douglas MacMillan. "'Doomed to Fail': Why a $4 Trillion Bailout Couldn't Revive the American Economy." The Washington Post. WP Company, October 5, 2020. https://www.washingtonpost.com/graphics/2020/business/coronavirus-bailout-spending/.

Made in the USA
Middletown, DE
15 May 2021

39786449R00099